STEVEN BURNS

SCRIBBLES

RANDOM THERAPEUTIC THOUGHTS

CONTENTS

SECTION 3 - SELF-AWARENESS

INTRODUCTION

This book is random. And it's meant to be. The reason for this is that "thinking" itself can often be quite random. As human beings we engage in strategic thinking, we run patterns of predictable thought. But so much of what goes on for us seems to come from a mysterious place outwith our conscious control. Strange ideas, opinions and perspectives can often bubble up from our subconscious in ways that feel random and difficult to intellectualise initially.

"Insight" can also be random. Unexpected. In fact, they aren't called "Aha!" moments for no reason. At the slightest moment we can be introduced to a new idea that can provoke us into thinking about life in a different way; one that allows us to see more of our own potential and what the world has to offer.

I remember reading once that we are only ever one "thought" away from a profound transformation, one shift in perspective away from seeing the world, and our role in it, in a significantly more enriched way. I think there's a lot of truth in this and find it beautifully comforting. As human beings we can change and develop in a multitude of ways. It can be quick, slow, painful, enjoyable, delightful. It can be instigated by our own conscious efforts or it can be forced upon on us from the outside, with a whole infinite spectrum of variations in between.

As a therapist, coach and trainer for close to 20 years, one of the aspects of change that has fascinated me the most is the kind that happens through sudden insight; a reflective moment where we examine our situation from a different angle, that causes us to change our honest assessment of it.

I've seen this happen time and time again during both one-to-one coaching and therapy sessions. You can work tirelessly, attempting to encourage people to change their thinking, with little in the way of success. Only to then ask a mildly provocative question towards the end of the session and it creates a shift within seconds.

There is method to this type of questioning of course, but, more often than not, as the coach or therapist, you have no way knowing for sure before-hand which question will make the difference.

For years I've been curious about what causes this. Is it because the client is utterly worn down by the constant badgering and just submits to the therapist's will?

Perhaps, but I don't think so.

I think a more revealing explanation is that by asking mildly provocative questions it encourages people to step into perspectives they most likely haven't stepped into before. It takes them **outside** their current world-view and encourages them to consider life from a different angle. Once they fully step into it in their imagination, life can no longer be viewed in the same way.

A similar thing happens with teaching, and also with writing. A teacher's job is not just to get students through an exam - even though they are under immense pressure nowadays to do so. Great teachers encourage deeper insight. They push students to question their reality, provoking inner reflection that can then lead to a richer understanding of the world.

A skilled writer doesn't just present information: they change the way you think. One of my own personal favourites is non-fiction writer Malcolm Gladwell. You could argue that his ideas aren't thoroughly researched

- by academic standards - but few can say that he isn't a master when it comes to encouraging you to view a different version of reality.

This form of change, for me, can be the most subtle, while at the same time being the most profound. When something is "thought-provoking" it jump-starts the process of inner re-evaluation and causes us to update our current way of viewing the world.

It's for this reason that I've decided to keep the structure of this book loose. A little bit random. It consists of a collection of "random transformational thoughts", ideas that will hopefully cause you to think differently about life. If you're looking for a "self-help system" that will lead you to a specific result, step-by-step, then you're in the wrong place. There is a time and place for systems of course, but my aim with this book is more to stimulate, encourage, and occasionally provoke inner reflection and re-evaluation. My objective is simply to be thought-provoking. The rest is up to you.

That being said, I did still feel that I had to appease the more structured side of my brain somewhat and arrange the chapters into some kind of coherent fashion. Even though they are designed to create random new insights into life, I do appreciate that structure and categorisation are important. Because of this, I've arranged the thoughts into 3 main categories: Achievement, Self-reflection, and Living life to the full. Please see these as loose distinctions. If they don't resonate with you then feel free to re-allocate them to a different category in your mind.

Each chapter - or "thought" - is brief: between 1000 - 1300 words. Think of them as "vignettes": short explorations into a subject or idea that are designed to make you think.

When I discussed the idea behind the book with my business partner we had a rather humorous exchange. He liked the idea but then went on to label it a "toilet book". Because of the short nature of each of the chapters, he said that it would be the perfect book to read while you were on the toilet. You could finish a chapter while you were "doing your business". I'm not sure how I feel about this comparison, and it's not particularly pleasant to picture potential readers semi-naked squatting over a pan, but I do understand why he made it. The chapters are brief so you can pick it up and quickly get something from them. You won't have to wade through pages and pages of filler content. I've done my best to make every sentence count.

You can, of course, read the book any way you like, but my recommendation is that you read a few chapters then pause to let the ideas settle – and, if you really must, you can do this on the toilet. Then, when you're ready, write down any insights that come to mind on a piece of paper. If nothing comes to mind immediately then that's fine, just let it sit for a little bit longer. That's often the way of "insight"; it happens first at the subconscious level and then eventually bubbles up to cognition.

We are so much more than we think, and I mean this in more ways than one. Firstly, we have vastly more potential than we think we have, and secondly, there is so much more to us than our conscious, cognitive thinking. Thought provocation and inner reflection, in my opinion, are wonderful ways to access more of each of these.

Enjoy the book. I do hope my scribbles will help you experience many random therapeutic thoughts.

SECTION 1

LIVING LIFE TO THE FULL

CHAPTER 1

THE MOMENT WHEN YOUR LIFE FLASHES IN FRONT OF YOUR EYES

"I've heard your entire life flashes in front of your eyes the second before you die".

I didn't write that to shock you. This is, in fact, part of the end monologue from the film American Beauty, directed by Sam Mendes.

I've discussed this film and its potential meanings with many friends and acquaintances and it tends to create polarised responses: they either find it hugely inspiring or disturbingly uncomfortable.

If you haven't seen it, it's a story about a man in his forties going through a mid-life crisis. He decides to quit his job, leave his stale, unfulfilling marriage and start appreciating each and every moment of life, in a similar way that he did when he was young.

I found it inspiring but I know it does raise big questions for people who have unhappily found themselves entrenched in the proverbial rat-race. It often leads them to question, uncomfortably, how their own life is panning out; if it's turned out the way they would have liked it to.

One of the interesting aspects of the film is that we know from the outset that the main character is going to die. This is made explicit in the first scene through the opening monologue. From there on the story is about how he gets to this endpoint and whether or not he can make his "final movie-reel" worthwhile.

It provocatively prompts the viewer to ask a similar question of themselves: **When your entire life flashes before your eyes the moment before you die will you like what you see?** Will you see something worthwhile and meaningful, or will it feel like a missed opportunity?

Whether or not you've seen the film the theme behind the question is a transformational one: the importance of making the most of the time we have. It's morbid but it's important to think about, especially as we get older.

So what about you? Are you spending enough time living the life you want? One that resonates deeply within you?

How is your final movie-reel currently shaping up? Is it looking like a well-crafted story with lots of meaningful moments? Or does it feel like someone with a sick sense of humour is writing the plot?

These are tough questions that can raise issues for people, but they are some of the most important ones that you can ask yourself.

The Psychologist Schopenhauer said that when you reach a certain point in your life, you can look back and it's almost as if your life has a plot to it; like it's been written by a skilled novelist. It has ups, downs, lulls and points of high drama. It might not seem like it when it's happening but, in retrospect, it's like it has its own story thread that evolves over time.

When you examine your own story, your own plot-line, how is it looking so far? And more importantly, in which direction is the plot heading?

Everyone's story is unfinished so where it goes from now is yet to be decided. Perhaps it will contain moments of drama, passion, meaning and transformation? Or maybe it'll just peter out like a novelist who runs out of ideas at the end of a book?

Which would you prefer? Not to be presumptuous but I would imagine that most would choose the first option. If that's you, then perhaps it's time to take hold of the pen more often.

Irrespective of whether we pay attention to it or not, and how much conscious influence we inject, our story will be naturally heading in a particular direction; by virtue of how we've lived our life in the past and how we're currently living it now. And if we don't take charge of the pen every now and again then who knows what kind of tale we'll end up with.

We don't often realise, but it is largely **us** that gets to choose which direction our story is heading in. We get the biggest say in how our final movie-reel will look. It's almost impossible to accurately predict all the details of our future, of course; there are too many variables and life can be wholly unpredictable, but we do get to write the plot-line most of the time. We do have a significant influence over the direction in which our plot-line is heading if we choose to take responsibility for it.

How much time do you actually spend plotting your own life's story; panning the camera back and taking a look at the direction in which you've been heading and where it's going from here?

You obviously can't go through life without commitments, and it's also important to enjoy the randomness of organic life, but how often do you actively engineer the path you're heading down? How much time do you spend plotting your own story?

So often we forget that we are the chief authors of our own lives. We can also have many co-contributors; people who add in new ideas, and external factors that cause occasional plot-twists, but **we** are the ones that get to hold the pen the majority of the time. Sometimes we can become so lost in life that we completely forget this but it's important to remind ourselves: we are forever in the process of creating our own personal story.

It's like what John Lennon once said. That, "life is something that happens to you when you're busy making other plans." Perhaps we should take this as a warning rather than a fact of life.

So, if you haven't already asked these - sometimes uncomfortable - questions, I'd like you to find the courage to do so now:

- In what direction is your story currently heading?
- And in what direction would you like it to head?

It doesn't matter what age you are (it's never too late) and it doesn't mean that you have to burn all your bridges and start again with a blank page. Most of the time, all that's required is a slight change in plot direction; a subtle tweak to the script.

You do have to be honest with yourself though. By virtue of the way you've been living your life up to this point, where is your story naturally heading? And is this what you want? If not then something has to change.

Maybe you **do** want a complete change in direction, a total reinvention. Or perhaps it's a more subtle change, like spending more time on your passions or having a greater sense of gratitude for the things that you already have. Whatever you choose, it's important to keep an awareness of your story direction, because the pen doesn't stop writing. The plot doesn't stop unravelling, even when we're busy doing other things. Because at the end of the day we will all have our own final movie-reel to watch.

When your life flashes in front of you the moment before you die, what will you see?

Will it be a beautiful piece of self-written genius or some dodgy B-movie with actors who clearly don't want to be there?

The beauty of it is: the choice is up to you.

CHAPTER 2

THE MORE YOU LOSE YOURSELF, THE MORE YOU FIND YOURSELF

Recently, one of my friends posted a photograph on Facebook. It was a selfie of him at a Radiohead concert with the caption: "Having the most amazing time here at the Radiohead concert!!"

He certainly looked like he was having an amazing time in the photo but I couldn't help shake the feeling that he had somehow missed the point of going to a concert.

Was he really **fully there** watching Radiohead? Or was he someplace else?

My thoughts were that he would get more pleasure from giving his full attention to the band rather than posting about it on social media. He might have been "physically" at the Radiohead concert but "mentally" he was on Facebook.

I don't know how often you do this yourself but it is a trend that's on the increase - commenting "about" our experience rather than connecting fully with it.

As human beings, we have a gift. We can be "in" our experience, fully committed to it, but we can also "step out" to think, reflect and consider other areas of our life. These modes are not mutually exclusive and we constantly float between them, depending on what we are doing. We need to step out and think, plan, analyse, consider and reflect; we need to float psychologically into the past, or dream about our future, in order to learn and decide which direction we're going to head in. But often we forget that much of the pleasure of life exists right in front of us. In the here-and-now. In the moment.

What my friend was really saying was that he was having an amazing time at the concert **posting about** Radiohead. Not **watching** Radiohead.

There is, of course, nothing necessarily wrong with this. Having a conversation about our experiences can be pleasurable. But to comment about a gig is not the same thing as fully immersing yourself in the wonders of live music, and it's the same with many other aspects of our day-to-day activity. The latter contains a different kind of pleasure that only presents itself when we commit fully to our experience; when we establish a deeper connection with our moment-to-moment reality and become immersed. By committing, and letting go fully into the dance of life, a whole world of pleasure and meaning becomes available to us that so often slips right by when we're busy thinking.

When you think about your own life do you find that this resonates? How often do you give your full attention to something? Where you lock-into what you're doing and immerse yourself, etching out every ounce of natural pleasure it has to offer? How often do you make it your goal to fully commit to experience?

It's interesting. It's an idea that we shouldn't have to remind ourselves of but we do. In the modern, fast-paced world we're continually encouraged to split our attention, defusing it to the extent where we rarely experience more than just a quick glance at multiple aspects of our reality.

Our jobs also often demand that we multi-task. There are few careers that don't have the knack of bewitchingly teasing us into attempting "the juggle" - trying to do a million things all at the same time. With the modern world set up in the way it is, it's no wonder that many people find it challenging to give a single activity their full attention: to commit to the experience. It's vitally important that we retain our ability to do so though. And to develop it, con-sistently, through practice. It's important that we make it a priority because the rest of the world won't - in fact, the rest of the world is trying to encourage us to do the opposite.

When we commit to experiencing more we re-capture a piece of what it was like to be a kid. We re-kindle a deeper connection with the world and start to appreciate more of the natural pleasure it has to offer.

Stop for a moment and think back to a time when you were fully immersed in what you were doing. Perhaps you were reading a book, going for a run, or enjoying an evening with friends? How did you feel during it? How did you feel after it?

Most people describe it as an almost euphoric moment, where they find a deep natural pleasure within the act of being immersed. And almost always this is then followed by an "after-glow", a warm fuzzy feeling of satisfaction and fulfilment that they bask in when the activity is over. There's something quite profound about fully connecting with the moment, and it's vital that we bring it more to the forefront of our lives.

Committing to experience can also help us be more of our true selves. There's something innately liberating about letting go into the moment: **the more we lose ourselves the more we tend to find ourselves**.

To do this can also considerably reduce stress. So much of stress these days is caused by over thinking; trying to manage a quite ridiculous number of concerns in our mind. "Overwhelm" is often where we stack multiple different important considerations on top of each other in our mind and attempt to address them all at the same time. It's not possible, but we often attempt to do it anyway and the repercussions can be extremely harmful to our mental and physical state.

Giving each activity our full attention before moving on to the next can reduce stress considerably, and make life a lot more enjoyable. It's like the age-old advice that my granny used to tell me: "You can only ever do one thing at a time".

This isn't something you hear too frequently nowadays, but it's more relevant than ever. There's a simplicity to experience that we often forget: where we just connect with the moment and allow it to take us. Then, once we're finished, we move on to the next. Whether it be writing, reading, doing exercise, having fun with friends, watching a movie, speaking with a client, giving a presentation, or something else, when we give it our full attention life becomes simpler, easier and more enjoyable.

So in this thought, I'd like to encourage you to commit to experiencing more. Make it a regular goal. Be "in" life rather than on the outside looking in. It's much better to be the main protagonist of a story than a critic of it.

Also, do your best to minimise diffusing of attention. I know it's difficult because most people - myself included - have excessive demands and responsibilities placed on them both personally and professionally. And most of us own multiple different electronic devices that follow us around, constantly pinging away, trying to demand our attention. That's why we have to make it a goal and regularly remind ourselves of it. Life demands that we split our attention over multiple different sources so it's crucial that we make an attempt to do the opposite. There's a life right in front of you and you might well be missing it because you're not giving it your full attention.

It won't be possible to do it all the time, of course. We still have to psychologically "step out" to reflect, analyse and think about other areas of our life, and the world still requires us to multi-task, to a certain degree. But, whenever you can, make it a priority to commit and immerse yourself in experience and I promise you'll be happier as a result.

You'll find more meaning, pleasure and enjoyment than you can contend with. Because the more you lose yourself, the more you find yourself.

CHAPTER 3

SEEING THE WORLD IN 4K

One of the most profound things we can do is to see the world in full resolution.

A few years ago - after going through a long period of denial - I forced myself into getting an eye test. I had squinted one too many times at road signs. I had mistaken strangers for friends, and friends for strangers, for the last time. So I bit the bullet and went to the local opticians.

I know it's just a natural part of the ageing process but I found it hard to do. It's like an admission that your body is starting to fail you. After an hour of tests, I emerged as the proud owner of a lovely pair of designer prescription specs. More importantly though, I could see.

As I drove back from the opticians I was struck by how different the world looked. What used to be a slightly faded, blurry approximation was now sharp, detailed and focused.

Looking at the nearby scenery, the thought that was going through my mind was, "Okay, so this is what it's like to see the world the way it's meant to look! This is what it's like to see the world in its full resolution."

I stopped the car close to my house and spent at least 10 minutes staring at a tree. It was beautiful and detailed. How had I not acknowledged this before? I was taken aback by all the subtle refinements that I'd been missing and how hypnotically picturesque it looked. The reality was though, that it had always been this beautiful and detailed: I just hadn't seen it in its true form for some time. I had been looking, but not **really** seeing.

How often does this happen in life, where we look at something but don't really see it? And I'm not talking about eyesight, I'm speaking metaphorically. I'm talking about looking beyond the initial first glance and fully connecting with experience at a deeper and more profound level.

As we explored in the last chapter, in the modern, high-paced world we are encouraged to skim. We have so much information to contend with, things to do and people to see, that we often don't take the time to stop and examine something for a longer portion of time: to appreciate depth instead of just the surface level appreciation.

It's important that we take the time to look deeper though: to explore beyond the surface and see what additional layers of pleasure and meaning are contained within our experiences. This starts with committing more to experience, and it continues when we look beyond the surface towards the additional layers of pleasure and meaning contained within everything we do.

If we don't look beyond the superficial then we miss out on much of the beauty that life has to offer. I missed out on the true beauty of a tree - mainly due to poor eyesight but also because I never stopped to look - so I wonder what else I've missed out on.

Every activity that we engage in, every person we interact with, and every material object we collect has more potential for meaning and pleasure than we realise. It's only when we stop and take the time to look that we start to see the additional layers; that we see the world in more of its full resolution.

Take something as simple as a movie. I remember the first time that I watched the film *Pulp Fiction*. I hated it. I went to the cinema to see it when I was 19 and just didn't get it at all. I'd heard all the reviews and acclaims of creative brilliance but the only thing that I was thinking as I walked out of the cinema was how boring and pointless I thought it was.

The scenes were too long, it was dialogue heavy and it didn't appear to have a coherent structure; John Travolta gets shot dead halfway through the film and then miraculously appears in another scene right after it. I had absolutely no idea what was going on.

It wasn't until a few years later, when I watched it for a second time as a more mature adult, that I realised why the scenes were arranged in the way they were; they weren't actually meant to be shown in chronological order and the film had a deliberate and quite innovative structure.

As I watched it through older and wiser eyes, I suddenly appreciated its brilliance: the acting, the dialogue and the quirky atmosphere Tarantino had created. It was utterly absorbing.

Why on earth hadn't I noticed it the first time around? Why hadn't I seen and appreciated the genius?

In hindsight, my guess is that the genius had always been there: I just needed to look a little beyond my initial, immature first glance.

And this is just a movie. What if **everything** we engage in, in life, has the potential to offer more meaning and pleasure than what we realise?

The friends and colleagues we interact with, the

activities we engage in, the cars, houses and toys we buy. If that was the case, surely it would be a crushing shame not to take the time to explore and connect with these additional layers?

It puts a very different spin on the definition of "living an abundant life", which is often one of the key goals of self-help. Abundance is often thought of as "having more" in terms of quantity, but what if **true** abundance was actually the appreciation of the multiple layers of meaning and pleasure contained within the few? It would mean that no matter what our life situation, we could experience abundance in some capacity.

It doesn't mean we that we can't pursue more of what we want. We can still spend our hard earned cash on luxurious possessions if we desire, and we can still travel to multiple different holiday destinations if that's what takes our fancy. It just means that we can appreciate more. We don't necessarily need an abundance of things to feel fulfilled and happy. We are able to connect with more of the pleasure and meaning that each individual experience has to offer because we are willing to take a second look: to properly see.

It's an interesting thought and one that can be

transformational. We live in a time where - assuming you live in a reasonably affluent area - we have a plethora of choice, but somehow, many manage to pull off the trick of being miserable and unhappy. Well, perhaps it's time to stop accumulating and to start looking?

To properly look and peer beyond the surface level appreciation of the many and start to connect with the depth of meaning in the few. There's potentially a whole world of pleasure in there that you might be missing.

So in this chapter, I'd like you to take the time to consider all the different areas of your life and become curious about the additional layers of appreciation they may contain.

What aspects of your life do you think would merit a second, third or even fourth glance?

Which areas, activities, people or objects are worth exploring in more depth?

What additional layers of meaning and pleasure are you currently missing out on?

You can even make a list if you like.

Some aspects of your life won't be worth the additional attention but I guarantee there will be some that contain hidden gems that haven't been found yet. It's worth looking for them.

Because by looking longer and closer we can start to truly see: to see the world more in its full resolution.

CHAPTER 4

WHAT IF YOU GAVE YOURSELF PERMISSION?

What would it be like if you were to give yourself permission? Permission to let loose, to express yourself, to be more of your raw, uninhibited self without fear of social recrimination. Permission to "just be".

As human beings we all have a relationship with "rules": regulations, guidelines, dos and don'ts and encouraged social norms. They're everywhere. If we want to be part of a civilised society we must, to a certain degree, play by the rules and exist within a structured framework. Even if you're someone who likes to push the boundaries and challenge the status quo, this fact will still be part of your reality; we have to accept that rules exist and that breaking them could potentially lead to disapproval, recrimination, or even punishment.

And as a society, we need this. Without personal and social rules we would most likely descend into anarchy.

We need structure, and the safety that this provides.

Rules also restrict us though. They can prevent us from having free reign to do what we like and behave in ways that satisfy our deepest urges and desires, and this can be highly frustrating. We see some rules as fair and others as unjust and restrictive

As members of a society, we often look outwards to the rules, regulations and guidelines laid down by politicians, parents and organisations as the reasons we can't be free and unrestricted as a person. But the rules that often slip passed unnoticed are those we impose on ourselves: the shoulds and should-nots that restrict how we behave, and what we believe we can do and achieve as a person.

It's important to examine external rules laid down by others, of course, and fight against injustice, but it's equally - if not more - important to examine the internal rules we live by. To look out for those that throttle our potential for happiness, freedom, creativity and success. We all have destructive "inner rules" that we have unwittingly subscribed to and one of the most liberating things we can do is to step into a place beyond them.

These inner rules are often unconscious too but that doesn't mean they don't affect us. In fact, it's usually the opposite. Because they sit somewhere deep inside of us, we mistake them for wisdom: an inner truth that's a complete depiction of reality. We've also invested in them because, essentially, we are the ones who have chosen to subscribe to them.

To bring one of these inner destructive rules into your conscious awareness just think of a highly ambitious goal, one that you'd like to achieve but you think is beyond your capabilities. When you imagine having this "out-of-reach goal" what happens? Usually, we create a picture of it inside our mind and then, all of a sudden, a little inner-voice pops up and tells us, unequivocally, that we're not good enough; that it's not possible for us. It's your voice by the way, and it's actually doing its job correctly. It's just a vocal expression of an inner rule that you've subscribed to.

Another example could be an inner rule that hinders your self-expression: Have you ever felt like you couldn't express yourself properly in certain situations? That you couldn't let the world see **who you really are**? Perhaps it's at work, with a certain circle of friends, or just socially in general.

When we feel that we are inhibited as people we often

attribute this responsibility solely to the environment we find ourselves in. This can play a big part, of course, but what's often more significant is what's going on inside of us; the rule we've internalised and are now playing out.

Think about it. Unless you're being forcibly coerced into not being yourself then it's you who is choosing to do it. It might be in response to the environment you find yourself in, and there's a high chance it's happening outwith your conscious awareness, but it's still an internal idea that you are subscribing to. You're not alone though, and it's something everyone has to deal with. We all have destructive internal rules that affect our potential for success, self-expression, creativity, happiness and - ultimately - our capacity for living a meaningful and worthwhile life.

That's why it's so important to give yourself permission every now and again; permission to let go of any ideas you might have of what you should or shouldn't do. You don't have to stay there forever, you just have to re-connect with it every now and again.

We all need to have an inner code of conduct; an inner compass that makes sure we don't deliberately hurt or harm other individuals. We also all have to take on a "role" every now and again. To read our environment and be flexible is a vital skill, but a problem arises when we confuse the role with who we really are; when the inner code of conduct becomes an excuse for not being who we want to be deep down; when we forget that a social mask is just that - a mask. It's important that we occasionally step into a place beyond this, and re-connect with the unrestricted, creative buzz bomb that's inside each and every one of us.

By giving yourself permission to "just be", it allows you to bypass your inner destructive rules; the restrictive stories that you tell yourself that severely limit your behaviour and potential. When we give ourselves permission to let loose, to let the world see our raw, uninhibited self, it lights a beautiful fire within us. It awakens a place of creative expression that can be quite intoxicating, both for us and the people we interact with.

One of the things I love to do is improvisation classes. As someone who generally likes to have structure in their life, the thought of "winging it" and "going with the flow" in an improvisation class triggered considerable anxiety at first. After the initial wobble though, I realised how wonderful this unregulated place can be. It's a place of unrestricted creativity: a place where you are free to explore "You".

In a world filled full of rules - both internal and external - there's something profoundly therapeutic about this. Giving ourselves permission can be like this: where we let go of any internal restrictions we've placed on ourselves and simply explore what's left. What energetic presence is beyond all the rules that you think you have to adhere to?

For further exploration you can use the following question frame:

"What would it be like if you were to give yourself permission to {fill in the blank}?"

I find this a wonderfully transformational frame of mind to reflect on every now and again.

The rules we impose on ourselves can often slide in unnoticed, but by asking this simple question - and then adapting it to suit different goals - we can step into a blissfully free place beyond them.

"What would it be like if you were to give yourself permission to be successful?"

"What would it be like if you were to give yourself permission to love?"

"What would it be like if you were to give yourself

permission to enjoy life fully?"

And my own personal favourite:

"What would it be like if you were to give yourself permission to be your uninhibited self?"

For me, when I reflect on this last one it produces a feeling that's quite profound. A weight of social expectation lifts off my shoulders and I feel a sense of pure freedom of expression. It's wonderful.

Again, of course, we need structure and regulation, but I do think it's possible to live in the world of rules while at the same time regularly connecting with our own unique, creative selves. It's not necessarily an "either or" choice. The two can co-exist in some shape or form.

So what would it be like if you were to give yourself permission to {fill in the blank}?

Go ahead and give it a go. But of course, you don't need my permission: only your own.

CHAPTER 5

WHAT'S YOUR CREATIVE EXPRESSION?

As a bit of a follow-on from the previous thought, I'd like to ask: **what's your creative expression?**

For years I used to think that "creative expression" was something that only those involved in the arts were concerned with. It was the slightly weird thing that you did in drama class at school when your teacher asked you to pretend to be a tree. Or the apple that you attempted to draw - badly, in my case - in art class.

I think one of the biggest realisations we can make is that "creative expression" is for everyone. And it can be one of the most important things we do as a human being. It goes so much further than drama, theatre and art.

When you read a self-help book, you often hear the mantra, "just be yourself", like it's some kind of cure-all for every known psychological angst. If we could just let go of the need to socially conform and break through the psychological restrictions we place on ourselves in order to "just be our true self" then all of life would be fine.

And it's true; it would make a difference. As we mentioned in the last thought, social conformity is necessary, to a certain degree, but it's also important to step into a space where we can let loose; to give ourselves permission to be ourselves. And, ultimately, this is all about self-expression.

When a self-help guru - or a well-meaning friend for that matter - tells you that you should, "just be yourself", what they are **really** saying is that you should creatively express yourself more: let the world see the unique and creative entity that is you.

When you take your inner-most thoughts, ideas, experiences, and more resonant aspects of your personality, and allow the world to see them, you are creatively expressing yourself in a way that will be unique to you. You are letting the world see your inner personality; the one that exists behind the need to socially conform.

This is so fundamentally important to us as human beings but something many people overlook. Whether it be socially through your sense of humour, in the work-place through your communication style, in the home as a parent, or as a business owner through your products and services, your actions and creations will contain parts of who you are. By giving yourself more free-reign to express them, you're giving people a glimpse into your inner world while at the same time contributing to theirs. And there's something quite profound about that.

This is one of the reasons why I love being a business owner. It's hard work and certainly doesn't offer the freedom that people often think it does; but it does offer greater potential for creative expression. I think that's why it can be so meaningful. You're not just offering a service or product, you're letting the world see a piece of your personality.

In any job or career, there is the potential to express yourself - with some careers offering more potential than others, of course. The activities you engage in might be decided by someone else, like your boss, but the way you go about these activities is largely up to you. We all have our own "styles" and it's important to embrace them, and let them out more.

If you're a geek, embrace it. If you're super-smooth, embrace it. If you're a wacky professor-type like Doc from *Back to the Future*, then embrace it. It's not all of who you are, of course, but if it resonates then it's an important part worth letting out.

I know this can be scary because, often, when we were kids in the playground, "being different" led to teasing and ridicule. But as an adult, it's not the same. We have higher thresholds for difference so by embracing our creative expression we stand out from the crowd and therefore become more attractive. This will always come with a certain degree of risk, of course, but the rewards - both personally and professionally - can be colossal. You won't appeal to everyone but you'll find your people. You'll resonate with similar personality types and connect with those that are right for you. Plus, more people get to see the value that you have to offer which almost always leads to richer opportunities.

It's often when we go against our own styles and fight with them, that they become strange to others. When you own it and go with it, people generally start to see it as engaging and endearing.

I remember when I was learning to dance Cuban-style Salsa about 7 years ago, my teacher kept talking about the importance of developing your own style as a dancer. He emphasised time and time again that all truly engaging styles come "through" the dancer: It's not something they put on, it's a reflection of their personality. So if you are an outgoing person then you dance larger; if you are more reserved then you might have a more subtle style.

You can gain insight and inspiration from other dancers of course, and attempt to emulate, but it's important that their styles resonate with your character, or the dance just doesn't look right. It's an "inside-out" process as well as an "outside-in" one.

In Cuba, they call this quality "sabor", which is Spanish for "flavour" or "taste". It's one of the main reasons that they dance. It's not just about moving their body in quite beautifully hypnotic ways, it's about letting the world see their style: their creative expression.

So what is your flavour? What is your sabor? What's your creative expression?

And perhaps it's time to let the world see it a bit more. Don't fight it. Let it out.

CHAPTER 6

A SERIES OF SMALL, BLISSFUL MOMENTS

I remember reading a story about a man who had been in prison for 15 years. When he finally got out he described his first month of being a free man as "a series of small blissful moments".

Perhaps it was having a glass of fine wine, watching a film, spending time with his family, or going for a walk in a forest; the experiences he described were small and simple yet they seemed to affect and move him in a way that was intoxicatingly beautiful. He said it was like becoming a child again: that he had somehow managed to recapture the innocent wonder of life he had left behind several decades ago.

Being locked away in a prison had brought the beauty of the simple things in life rushing back to the forefront of his mind. It gave him the gift of perspective. Aspects of life he would never previously have considered sources of pleasure, suddenly held a tremendous amount of meaning and value.

It's a shame he had to go through 15 years of pain to discover this but at least he caught a glimpse of it; at least he had the brief experience of re-connecting with the pleasure and meaning that can be found in the potentially infinite number of day-to-day small and simple things.

Unfortunately, I don't know any more of his story so I've no idea if it was life-transformational or not, but I do think that there's an important lesson to be drawn from his experience: that sometimes in life thinking small can be a good thing.

Now, this is not self-help advice you'll often hear. We're generally led to believe that the definition of success and happiness is to think - and achieve - big all the time.

"Think **big**, make a **massive** impact, awaken the **giant** within you, **maximise** your productivity, achieve your **enormous** potential".

These are common sound bites and I could list many more, but I think you probably get the picture. The **big** picture. The **huge** picture. The **colossally gargantuan** picture.

The personal development world can be a bit "size-ist". The emphasis is so firmly focused on the scale and size of our achievements that the smaller moments can regularly get lost in the noise. The idea that something small, and seemingly insignificant, could actually be deeply meaningful and worthwhile often gets forgotten.

When we are continually striving to create and achieve bigger and more impressive results, egged on ferociously from the stands by countless self-help books and self-improvement systems telling us that we should be "thinking big" all the time and achieving worldwide acclaim, it's all too easy to create a notion of happiness and success that doesn't include the small stuff; one that omits the more subtle, day-to-day sources of pleasure that are available to experience right now, in this very moment.

As we're off building businesses, striving for promotion after promotion, increasing our bank accounts, maximising our Facebook likes, or daydreaming that one day we could be in a lofty position of power and influence, we can give ourselves amnesia to all the smaller sources of pleasure existing right on our door-step. Either we just don't see them, magically deleting them from our conscious awareness, or we start believing that, by virtue of their smaller size, they simply aren't worthy of recognition.

When this happens it's a real shame. It's also a big

mistake. So much of our life will be made up of smaller moments so to devalue them is a huge error of judgement. We need to elevate their importance and connect with them more. If we don't then we risk missing out on a significant source of pleasure and meaning.

Of course, I'm not suggesting that thinking - and achieving - big is not a good thing. It is. To be ambitious and have the goal of creating something of huge significance is an aim I think we should all aspire to. It's highly enriching to work on a project that could have a huge impact; it's thrilling and meaningful. Just don't buy into the idea that achieving big is a pre-requisite to a happy and fulfilling life.

When we buy into this common self-help mantra, it can make us continually more oblivious to the subtle pleasures life has to offer. If we're not careful, dissatisfaction can become a daily habit. Frustration can increase only to be temporarily relieved every now and again when we make some kind of big breakthrough in our career or personal life. We compare ourselves to celebrities, successful entrepreneurs or social influencers with massive cyber-followings, and dream that one day we'll strike it gold and become as big as they are.

Before we know it, achieving big and becoming significant becomes like a drug that we need in order to not feel a failure, rather than the pleasure and thrill it's meant to be.

I'm sure I don't have to convince you of this though, as the evidence is all around you to see. We live in a world of great excess yet so many people still struggle to find happiness from it; regularly living from a place of dissatisfaction, stress and anxiety, never really feeling like they have "enough" to experience any kind of satisfactory level of fulfilment.

I think one of the best and most brutal places to see this in action is the TV show *X-Factor*. Year after year you see an assembly line of hopeful contestants attaching nearly every bit of their self-worth, value and dignity to becoming a success on the big screen. Some make it but, as is witnessed every year, most end up being totally crushed, as their hopes of living the life of their dreams are shattered with one cutting remark from one of the judges - at least until next year, when they can go through the whole torturous process again in full view of a voyeuristic nation.

It's great entertainment, but I'm not convinced it's great for the mental health of the participants. It might seem like they're entering into a healthy belief system of achievement, where they are being encouraged to "actualise their big life dreams", but the reality is far from it; they are entering into one built on the silent assumption that success and happiness only comes when we achieve something external on a gigantically grand scale.

It's good to think big but it can be damaging and unhealthy to make achieving it an unconditional pre-requisite for happiness. And it's just simply not true either.

So when you think about your own life, how much attention do you place on thinking small as well as big?

If you were to elevate the importance of the smaller, more subtle aspects of your life so that your day becomes a series of small blissful moments, what would that be like?

It's a counter-intuitive idea but one that I think can be profoundly transformational. If you think about it, by sheer numbers alone, most of your life will be made up of these smaller, less eye-catching, moments so surely it makes sense to allocate more importance to them? They all add up. They all count.

With their volume, I'd suggest that doing this will actually end up adding more happiness and fulfilment to your life than the big achievements ever will.

We live life mostly at the micro level so it's important that we value these more subtle, everyday experiences; that we do our best to make the most out of them.

If you like, you could even make a list. Here are a few from my own list, if you're looking for inspiration:

Going for a walk; watching the sunset; enjoying a cup of hot tea in the morning; truly connecting with a friend; playing a round of golf; taking a day off to do nothing; basking in a hot bath; drinking a glass of fine red wine; climbing a hill; enjoying good food; playing a video game; spending time with family; going to the cinema; reading a book.

None of these are colossally big experiences or achievements; they're simple, basic activities. But they do still all contain considerable potential for pleasure and meaning.

The more you appreciate the simple, basic and smaller things in life - elevating their importance - the more you exercise your ability to appreciate life in general. You can still keep thinking big of course. Just don't forget to also think small, for that's where most of our experience is. Because when you do, it opens up the possibility for life to become a series of small blissful moments. And that's an awesome place to be.

CHAPTER 7

BE A CREATURE OF DIFFERENCE

How much unfamiliarity are you comfortable with? Are you a creature of comfort that clings to a metaphorical security blanket, surrounding yourself with what you know? Or do you crave difference and seek it out like a possessed thrill-seeker?

The relationship you have with both familiarity and difference is more important than you might think. In fact, I'd argue that your development and sense of security as an individual depends on it.

I recently listened to a podcast by New York Times journalist and author Malcolm Gladwell called, *Revisionist History*. It's a majestic example of storytelling and I'd thoroughly recommend you listen to it.

In one of his episodes Gladwell talks about "social thresholds": the idea that, as human beings, we are pressured into acting a particular way depending on how our peers are acting. Some people will have low thresholds, and be readily influenced, whereas others have high thresholds and will feel more comfortable engaging in actions and activities that perhaps conflict with the ideals of their peer group.

One example he gave was of 60s basketball star Wilt Chamberlain. Chamberlain was a legend of the sport with one flaw in his game: he couldn't shoot free throws. He was hopeless at them. So in 1962, he took the radical decision to change his free throw style to underarm. It fixed his problem to the extent that he went from being one of the worst free throwers in the league to one of the best.

All good, right? Well, actually, no.

Instead of sticking with the change that had clearly been successful, he decided to switch back. What happened next was predictable: he went back to being terrible at free throws.

Why did he do this? What possible reason could he have for blatantly ignoring his obvious improvement?

Well, apparently, it was because he was embarrassed. He didn't want to be seen by his peers to be doing - what is referred to in the sport as - a "granny shot". Underarm throws weren't for professionals; they were for people who didn't have the ability to throw over arm.

Gladwell goes on to make the point that, even when changing to something different is clearly the best choice, many people will still stick with the familiar: sometimes smart people do dumb things. And they don't do it because they've temporarily become stupid. They do it because they've reached their peer pressure threshold and can't stop themselves.

We all have our own social thresholds; those with low ones will cave quickly when faced with outside pressure whereas those with high ones will do their own thing regardless.

I don't know if you can relate to this but I certainly can. Since my early 20s, I've generally gone off in my own direction irrespective of whether it fits with social expectations. It's not that I've been disrespectful of how other people think and act - and I'm not immune to peer pressure by any means -, it's just that I disliked the idea of other people choosing my path.

One particular example is dancing, which I learned to do in my early 30s. In the UK, if you're a man and you dance, it's generally thought of as feminine; it's not something that a man is "supposed" to do.

When I first started learning to dance my friends found

it hilarious. They regularly ribbed me about it - In fact, I found out that they apparently spent a whole evening laughing at Facebook photos of me dancing Cuban style salsa with my dance partner. I could see the funny side of it - I was wearing a bright red shirt with a flamboyant open collar - but a part of me found it a little bit sad. Just because I was doing something that wasn't considered "the social norm" within my peer group, it was deemed to be ridiculous; embarrassing even.

How restrictive is that? To allow your peer group to decide what activities you should or shouldn't do. Extremely, I'd say. But more importantly, it's also a belief system that can have a significant detrimental effect on your ability to live a meaningful life.

We all experience social pressure, and we are all affected by it to a certain degree. We've also got our own social thresholds: our own personal limits where we stop exploring difference and stick with what's expected of us, or what's familiar. But to let this pressure stop us from expanding our world by having different experiences is a colossal mistake and one that can seriously affect our development and ability to be a resourceful person.

As human beings, we are pre-programmed to pay

attention to both familiarity and difference.

Familiarity - or sameness - because we need to know that our environment is safe. With "something that we know" we have evidence as to whether it's safe or not so we can exist in a place of comfort without having to be on alert for potential unknown threats. Familiarity gives us a base level of safety and security.

But we are also pre-programmed to spot and seek out difference. If we just stayed with what we knew, ultimately, we would perish. How would we find new opportunities to grow, develop and make our environment safer? In pre-historic times, if we didn't continually look to grow, other species would have taken our spot on the evolu- tionary ladder and hunted us down. I probably wouldn't be writing this on my lightning fast MacBook Pro.

Nature's way of forcing us to continually evolve was to make us bored in the presence of too much familiarity and give us an insatiable itch to explore uncharted territory. To use a cheesy sci-fi quote, "to boldly go where no man has gone before".

It's the human condition. We evolve through continual exploration into the unknown in an attempt to find more useful and meaningful ways of existing. We are driven by the continual desire to turn the "unknown" into the "known".

Which brings me back to social thresholds. To stick with "what's expected of you by your peer group" is to side with the familiar; the safe option where you blend into the crowd and do what the herd say you should do. To pursue your dreams, desires and what uniquely fits with you is often to do what's not expected, to do what's different. So there could be a conflict - between what you want and what your social world expects you to do. And is that a bad thing? Sometimes. But most of the time I don't think it is. It's often an indication that what you're doing is a good fit for you.

Now I'm not suggesting, of course, that you deliberately go against the social grain just for the sake of it. This is not about becoming an outsider. We all need a base level of familiarity to feel safe and secure and this is especially relevant when it comes to our social well-being. But we shouldn't let our social thresholds restrict us from continually enriching our world. If you want to do something, do it.

In fact, one of the best pieces of advice I've ever been given came from a colleague about 15 years ago. He said, "Do as many different things, with as many different people, in as many different places as you possibly can". To do this, you don't have to go to the extreme and emigrate to a different country. You just have to introduce as much difference into your life as you can handle.

Try learning a new language. Learn to dance. Go on holiday to somewhere you've never been before. Learn a new skill. Interact with groups of people you think are weird. Make new friends. Expand your boundaries. The list can be endless.

It's tempting to only stick with what's familiar, with what we know. But to do so is a sure-fire way to create brain boredom; a one-way ticket to stagnation. It might feel comfortable and safe in the moment but the detrimental effect over a longer period of time can be significant.

The more different experiences we can introduce into our lives, the more resourceful we will become, and the greater our capacity will be for experiencing an enriched life. By engaging in actions and activities that are different from what we would consider to be our norm, we switch on previously unexplored aspects of our mind. We become better, more resourceful and more grounded people. It seems like such a simple piece of self-help advice but - when applied - it can be one of the most profound.

Exploring difference leads to a better, more fulfilled life.

So what about you? Is your own social threshold preventing you from expanding your world?

Have you ever done what Wilt Chamberlain did? Attempt to change by doing something different, only to fall back into old patterns because of what's expected of you?

If so, perhaps you want to change that. Maybe it's time to sprinkle in some "difference", irrespective of what other people think.

There's a lot at stake, after all. Exploring difference is fundamentally important to living a meaningful and enriched life. You give up a lot when you stick with what's safe and familiar all the time.

If you were to pick one new activity to add to your life, that's starkly different from what you currently do, what would that be?

Or to take it even further:

What activities would you like to engage in that you think people might laugh at you for?

The fact that you secretly want to do them suggests that it's something you should do. If people laugh, let them. When you experience a deep sense of enrichment, as a result of doing it, you'll get the last laugh.

Ultimately though, don't be a creature of comfort that clings to a metaphorical security blanket; be a creature of difference. It's in your nature.

SECTION 2
ACHIEVEMENT

CHAPTER 8

WHAT'S YOUR WATERSHED MOMENT?

I'd like to ask you a question:

What's your watershed moment?

If you've read any self-help books then I'm sure you will have heard the - now rather clichéd and overused - story of Roger Bannister: In May 1954 he did, of course, become the first person to break the 4-minute mile.

Up until that point it was thought to be a feat that was beyond the scope of human capabilities, but on a track in Oxford, over 6 decades ago, Bannister turned the impossible into the possible; he turned a "can't" into a "can do".

Bannister's story is often told as a tale of success despite the odds, but it also highlights the power of possibility; what we can do when we don't actively restrict ourselves by placing false limits on our potential.

Breaking the 4-minute mile was, of course, a remarkable feat, but what was arguably more remarkable was the number of runners who broke it in the years that followed.

This - once impossible - goal has now been broken by over 1,400 male athletes and is now considered the standard for elite runners. Bannister effectively highlighted an option that people before him didn't believe was available; a choice that most didn't even think was on the menu. As soon as it became a possibility though, more and more runners achieved it.

This is an example of a watershed moment; as the dictionary definition says, "An event or period marking a turning point in a situation".

When you look back into your own past, what watershed moments have you personally experienced? And, more importantly, what ones will you engineer in the future?

Watershed moments don't have to be quite as dramatic as global sporting achievements but they will always contain a high level of importance. From a personal development perspective, they are moments in our life where we do something significant and the game suddenly changes; where we step over a threshold and the world becomes a different place. New opportunities open up, our personality shifts a little, our outlook on life changes, and we undergo profound personal transformation.

There are many different types but, ultimately, the

content of them will depend on the individual. For some, a watershed moment could be leaving their job. For others, it could be finally getting a job or holding one down for more than a month! It's entirely down to the individual. Our personal watershed moments can also often appear insignificant to others even though they are, in fact, deeply important to us.

Other examples could be taking that next step in your business by charging for your services, going for a promotion that you previously thought was beyond you, finally standing up to a bully, finishing a toxic relationship, or mending a broken one. There are countless variations but the underlying theme is that they mark a turning point in your life; a moment where you step over a threshold and drag your life up to a higher plane.

I'd argue that **any** ambitious goal or challenge that we face will contain, within it, several watershed moments: required actions that involve taking that quivering, uncertain step into uncharted territory; activities that involve us stepping over an important, "game-changing' threshold.

And for ambitious goals, this step into the unknown is inevitable. As the saying goes, "if we always do what we've

always done then we'll always get what we've always got".
We have to be willing to do something different than what
we've done previously or we'll just be maintaining the
status quo. We have to expand who we are so that we
offer more than what we've offered before.

So if there was one thing that you could do that would
create a positive watershed moment for you, what would
that be?

Looking forward to your future, what threshold **must**
you cross to take your life to the next level?

This future watershed moment might seem small and insignificant to others but that doesn't matter. The most important
thing is that it symbolises a meaningful step for you.

It could also be something that you've been avoiding for
a while. Often watershed moments come with a certain
amount of fear and trepidation. Change is exciting but it
can also be scary.

Whether it's exciting, scary or a blend of both, there will
be something worth doing that will change the landscape
of your experience; a crucial action that will force you to
step up and expand who you are.

What might that be for you? And - writing provocatively
- when are you going to do it?

We all have our 4-minute miles; our own personal and professional thresholds that have the potential to act as profound watershed moments; pivotal experiences that shape the scope of what we believe we can achieve. They are inevitable if we want to develop and take our life to a new level.

What if you deliberately identified your own, and then went at them head on?

I'll hazard a guess and say that the borders you put around possibility will suddenly expand. You'll catch a greater glimpse of your full potential and become more resourceful than what you were previously. Life, as they say, will never be the same again.

So what is your next watershed moment? What must you do to take your life to the next level?

CHAPTER 9

THE DIFFERENCE BETWEEN AWARENESS & FOCUS

When it comes to achieving your goals have you ever thought about the difference between "awareness" and "focus"?

These terms are obviously subjective, and each person will have their own unique ways of explaining them, so here are my own definitions:

"Awareness" is a soft appreciation of something; a general acknowledgement of existence.

"Focus" is where we concentrate our attention intensely on an aspect of experience and bring detail more into the forefront of our vision.

"Awareness" generally has a wide and soft scope, whereas "focus" has a sharp and narrow one.

These two distinctions are important for many reasons but they're especially important when it comes to the process of goal setting & achievement. When we're looking to get more of what we want from life we inevitably set goals; we make predictions about our future and then set about making them a reality with all the vigour we can muster.

Goal-setting processes are widely publicised and are a mainstay in many a self-help book. The processes are quite straightforward and they are generally all based on a simple premise: in life, you get more of what you focus on.

This is generally true, but is this the full story? Is it as simple as that?

I don't think it is, and that's where the difference between "awareness" and "focus" comes into play.

I'm sure you've heard the old self-help adage, "Always keep your eye on the prize". It's a commonly dished out phrase to emphasise the importance of focusing intently and consistently on the "end state" of your goal; creating a picture in your mind of what it will be like once it's been actualised.

While this is certainly a nice and snappy sound-bite, there's a big problem with it:

It's terrible advice.

Well, terrible is probably a little harsh. More incomplete with a significant flaw.

When you "always keep your eye on the prize", you can end up becoming so pre-occupied with the "end state" of the goal that you miss many of the vital pieces in the here-and-now that are required to make the goal a reality. You create a kind of tunnel vision, fixated on a future projection, that can lead you to becoming blind to the many things in the present moment that can help you get to your destination ecologically and more effortlessly.

It's a bit like if you were to walk across a busy road. You fix your gaze on the other side intensely and never budge your gaze. You walk over - keeping your eyes on the prize - without paying attention to the cars and trucks flying by. Sure, you might get lucky and manage to get safely over to the other side, but your chances are greatly reduced because you aren't paying attention to the journey; the process.

It's a similar scenario with goal achievement. Rarely do we achieve goals in a straight line, especially the bigger, more ambitious ones. It can be like a zigzag. Messy. Random. Organic.

As well as setting our intentions and fixing goals & outcomes in our mind, we have to become adept at responding to what the world is offering us from moment-to-moment. It's not all about paying attention to the destination; focusing on the journey is also essential.

So instead of "keeping your eye on the prize" constantly, try the following: set a goal, focus on the end-state for a short while, but then let it drift into your "awareness". Let it settle into the background, allowing your attention to turn back to the here-and-now. Then concentrate as much of your "focus" on what you need to do to make the goal a reality. Allow the picture of the finishing line to sit in your "awareness" but engage your "focus" on what you must to do to get there.

I've found that this distinction can make a transformational difference. You trust the more sub-conscious parts of yourself to guide you towards your destination, while at the same time utilising your conscious focus to experience, and deal with, the demands of the journey. Every now and again you might want to bring the destination back into sharper focus: to review and make adjustments. But afterwards it's important to let this image transform back into a soft idea; allow it to drift back into your "awareness" and return to a hazy, yet inspiring vision. That way you'll become **guided** towards your goals as well as **pushing** yourself towards them.

So what meaningful goals would you like to become more aware of? And what actions and activities do you

need to focus your attention on to make these goals a
reality?

CHAPTER 10

WHO ARE YOU BECOMING?

One of my favourite old-school personal development gurus is - the now sadly deceased - Jim Rhon.

Rhon is known as the godfather of modern-day personal development and even boasts the impressive accolade of having originally trained Tony Robbins.

He had a lovely turn of phrase that he used when describing the benefits of goal setting. He would say that the achievement of the goal itself was often not the most important part of the process: the most important part was, **who** we are becoming as a result of going after the goal.

While it's good to go after our specific outcomes it can be quite limiting - and sometimes soulless - to view life as a continual to-do list. You set a goal, you attempt to achieve it, you set another, you attempt to achieve that. Rinse and repeat.

To take a tunnel-visioned approach like this can certainly yield results but it's missing something. To reduce the entirety of human achievement to a list of specific objectives lacks a certain romance. It's like dissecting a movie into individual scenes without appreciating the larger, and more important, plot arcs.

We don't always realise it but goals and outcomes are sub-sets of larger, more important processes, so to focus all of our attention at the coal-face can cause us to miss out on a deeper and more holistic experience of life. When we pan the camera back and lift ourselves out of specificity, new additional layers to the goal achievement process start to reveal themselves.

There are many but one of the most important is **how the pursuit of a goal alters your character.** Goals are not just isolated objectives: **they are catalysts for personal change.**

When we go after a goal or outcome, unless it's just a relatively simple task, it **will** start to change who we are. Generally, the more ambitious the goal, the more we will change, and this "change" is well worth keeping an eye on.

How often have you heard people say things like, "This job is turning me into someone I don't like!" or, "I don't like the person I've become!" This is often an indication that they weren't paying attention to how the goal was changing their personality while they were pursuing it.

It's important to assess how a goal might change us, both positively and negatively, and then to keep a basic awareness of this as we're heading towards it. The change will rarely be "negative-free" but it's important that we don't unwittingly take ourselves into a place we categorically don't like.

I remember a few years ago a friend accepted a job as an assistant head teacher in a primary school. She thought it was the right thing to do because it was seen as the natural progression for a teacher. She hated it. There was virtually no teaching - which was what she loved doing - and the job was more akin to a social worker. Your day consisted of taking flak from all angles and you had to make all manner of unpopular decisions for the supposed greater good. It was turning her into the type of person she didn't want to become. You've maybe heard this story before.

It's important that we have an awareness of where our path is taking us and how this is affecting our character and personality; this can then make it possible for us to minimise the changes that conflict with our values and maximise the ones that fit neatly with them.

Generally, if we choose a goal that forces us to grow, and one that is ecological, then it will be a catalyst for powerful, positive character transformation.

I think it's rare that we choose a goal - especially if it's an ambitious one - that doesn't affect our character in a multitude of ways, both negatively and positively, but if we pay attention to the effect it's having on us we can make sure we don't cross any red lines. And we can increase the chances of becoming a more resourceful, skilful and well-rounded person. We don't often realise it at the time, but goals are not just end points: they are milestones on the journey of becoming someone different.

Now, this doesn't mean that by pursuing a goal you become a completely different person. We don't ever replace our character; we build on it. By pursuing ambitious goals we **add** additional layers to our personality: more colour, depth and refinement. Hopefully, we become more resourceful, skilful, adaptable, flexible, knowledgeable, interesting and – ultimately - more valuable.

So the key question is this: What additional layers would you like to add to your character?

And what goals would allow you to naturally develop these?

You won't know for sure, of course, until you set off on the journey but it's well worth making an initial assessment and then paying attention to it as you progress.

Or perhaps there's a particular skill set that's crucial to you moving forward in life?

Is there a goal that would force - or encourage - you to learn that skill?

Because once you learn a skill you can potentially use it for life, not just in the achievement of the specific goal.

And, ultimately, how might all of that affect the person you are developing into?

To paraphrase the eloquent Jim Rhon:

"Just who are you becoming as a result of pursuing your goals?"

Consider it. It's important.

CHAPTER 11

IS YOUR LIFE EXACTLY THE WAY YOU IMAGINED IT WOULD BE?

One of the things I love to do most at the end of a day is to sit back and watch Netflix. Recently, after going through an 80s nostalgia fascination, I decided to watch *Back to the Future Part Two*. I remember being mildly obsessed with the film as a kid. Michael J. Fox, for me, was the epitome of "cool". Doc was mental but irresistibly engaging. And Biff – let's face it - was just an idiot.

If you're one of the few who have never seen the films they're about time travel; a crazy, mad-cap scientist and his guitar playing assistant invent a time machine and use it to correct the mistakes of the past and future. *Back to the Future Part One* is set in the past with the sequel being based mostly in the future - or, at least, one possible version of the future.

As the viewer, we're whisked off into the dizzy, futuristic heights of 2015 where the world has turned into some kind of high-tech dystopia. We have skate hoverboards, flying cars that run on garbage, a rich American Oligarch who lives in a huge tower hotel ruling through fear, and virtual reality that's so realistic it can be easily mistaken for the real thing. It's a fantastical scene that's beautifully created, and one I remember being mesmerised by as a kid.

As I watched the film as an adult though, I started to feel mildly disappointed. I thought, "sure, we have virtual reality and America is doing its best on the rich Oligarch front, but no matter how hard I look in the cockpit of my 2018 Ford Focus I can't see the button that makes it fly."

Annoying. But so often a true depiction of life.

Making predictions about the future like this is an interesting thing. It's one of the prime purposes of most sci-fi films but it's also one of the fundamental gifts we possess as a human being.

In order to create the kind of life we want, and to avoid as many unnecessary pitfalls as we can, we project into imagined future-based scenarios; play things out in our head with a host of different possibilities. By doing so it allows us to narrow our focus, change our path if need be, and zero in on the elements of life we believe are important to us.

How often do you go off into your imagined future and ponder what it might be like?

When you do, what do you see?

And, does this vision often become a reality?

Or do you end up - as I did after watching *Back to the Future* - feeling mildly disappointed when it doesn't turn out exactly the way you'd like it to be?

There's a common narrative in the world of Personal Development that says you can use your imagination to create your own future: to visualise it inside your mind and then set about creating a carbon copy of it in your outer world.

The narrative is that you can "design" every aspect of your destiny in minuscule detail. First, picture it in your mind's eye and then, through sheer force of will, make it your reality.

I do think there's something in this, and from my own experience, occasionally, this can be the case - you imagine something, take action and then create something in the external world that ends up pretty close to what you originally envisioned.

One personal example is when I set the goal of breaking the 21-minute mark for a 5K. I imagined the steps inside my mind, planned out my training regime, stuck to an eating plan and, after a couple of months, ran it in 20 minutes 54 seconds. What occurred, in reality, was eerily close to how I originally pictured it inside my mind. But then again that goal was highly specific and completely within my own sphere of influence. That's not something you can say about every goal.

What isn't in the common goal setting narrative is that, more often than not, especially when it comes to the bigger, more complex goals of our life, the reality is we only ever end up with a close approximation of what we initially imagined. In fact, sometimes it can be radically different and that's not necessarily a bad thing.

In much the same way that the writers of *Back to the Future Part Two* got some elements right and some wrong, when we design larger aspects of our future, like our career or relationship goals, most of the time a win is just simply getting something **close** to our designs. And personally, I think this is absolutely nothing to feel disappointed with. In fact, I'd suggest that it's in-line with how the world naturally works.

Life, by nature, is unpredictable, organic and - at times - chaotic. It's an unfair expectation to think that we can tame it completely, and make it conform to our every design and demand.

So I'd like to give you some advice that you won't often read in a self-help book: If you don't manage to create the **exact** future you imagine and want, then that's absolutely fine. Just do your best to create an **approximation** of it.

Outwith highly specific goals, the details aren't that important. The key thing is that you envisage a future that excites you, one that inspires you to take action. At the end of the day when you create your own future-based vision, unless you're the most gifted clairvoyant on the planet, it will only ever be an approximation. Every prediction we make will always, to a certain degree, be based on incomplete information.

We might get it accurate some of the time and that's great but, mostly, the main purpose of imagining a brighter future is to set a powerful direction. It's an intention that helps us activate resources; one that stimulates movement and makes us positively salivate when we look at it, inspiring us to move forward.

When you get down to it, is it really an issue if things don't work out exactly as you planned?

I used to think so - and I am still a little bit disappointed we don't have flying cars - but with the benefit of age and experience, I've changed my opinion. Providing my vision is moving me forward in a profound and empowering way I know I'll get lots of great stuff anyway. If it's close to 100% accurate to what I envisioned then great, that's a bonus, but it's not a pre-requisite to my happiness. And you never know, maybe there will be a surprise or two thrown in for good measure, that ends up being even better than my initial predictions.

So the next time you're setting a goal, imagine what it would be like to achieve it, but don't chain yourself to the details. Especially if it's a larger, more complex aim. Cut yourself some slack if your life doesn't end up being a carbon copy of what you initially planned. Maybe that's the way it's meant to be. Perhaps it's a good thing.

Enjoy the journey and appreciate the unexpected pleasures that the organic nature of life often provides. My prediction is that you'll be happier, more relaxed and more fulfilled because of it.

Maybe you'll get flying cars or maybe you won't. Who knows?

And that's often the hidden beauty of it all.

CHAPTER 12

THE DIFFERENCE BETWEEN SELF-BELIEF & KNOW-HOW

When it comes to being successful what do you think is more important to have?

Self-belief - the inner sense of certainty that you can succeed.

Or *know-how* - the required knowledge, skills and abilities to be successful in your chosen field.

In years gone by know-how was the essential quality to have: recognise the key skills you have to learn, and the relevant knowledge you need to acquire, and this will give you a decent platform to be successful. It won't guarantee it, of course, because you still need to get out there and make some noise but you'll have a solid base to work from.

With the colossal rise of the human potential movement in recent decades though, a new solution to success has been introduced that seems to be trumping all others: the notion of self-belief. The idea that unstoppable self-belief is the answer to all of life's problems and challenges; it's the magic elixir that will propel you towards glorious success, irrespective of your current situation, or how much know-how you have.

It's not just the self-help industry that promotes this idea. Go on Facebook and you'll see countless memes offering well-meaning sound bites telling you that, "all you need to do is believe in yourself and all will be fine". It's a general narrative that's been picking up steam for the last decade or so.

But is self-belief really the **key** element to success? Is it the quality that should be developed above all else?

I'd like to suggest that it isn't. It's certainly a good starter, and, providing it's linked to the amount of ability you have, it can help give you that extra edge, but on its own, it's not the most important quality to cultivate. If you're looking to create long-term sustainable success it's much more useful to focus on continually developing your know-how; on highlighting the crucial skills, abilities and knowledge that you need to acquire and then relentlessly pursuing them.

On August 26th, 2017, MMA star Conor Macgregor fought Floyd Mayweather. Most purists thought it was a freak show but it caught the imagination of millions, even non-fight-fans. Conor had never fought a professional boxing match in his life whereas Floyd is regarded as one of the best pound-for-pound boxers of all time, and was unbeaten. It was a total mismatch, yet many of Conor's supporters believed vehemently that he was going to win. That's really quite something when you consider it for longer than 5 seconds.

Conor is renowned for his unwavering self-belief and that seemed to be his ace card. The collective narrative was, that if he had enough self-conviction then he could surpass the colossal gulf in skill and experience. He lost, and a 40-year old Mayweather hardly looked like he broke sweat.

Many people believed that he did himself justice in that fight, but for anyone who knows boxing and could see beyond the hype, it was clear that the whole thing was a complete farce: a masterclass in promotion and manipulation of perception. All the self-belief in the world wasn't going to make up for the gulf in ability. This is an extreme example but I hope it makes a point: that self-belief on its own has its limits.

Believing in yourself can be extremely empowering. It can help you tap into more of your inner resources and can cause you to give off an air of supreme confidence. But when it's not a reflection of your ability it becomes a problem. In fact, in some cases when the disparity between your self-belief and ability reaches a certain level, it can become comical.

Promoting the idea that success is all about self-belief leads people to think that it's a pre-requisite to achievement; that they have to believe in something wholeheartedly **before** they can achieve it. So they wait...and wait... and wait...and wait...and often never even get started. The reality is though, that the majority of belief we have in ourselves comes **from** the experience of pursuing our goals; it comes from the knowledge, skill and ability that we develop on the journey. In other words: **it comes from our know-how**. To doubt yourself, especially in the beginning, is actually a natural and healthy part of the goal achievement process.

The exception to this is, of course, if you're a bullshitter. I'm sure we all have examples of people with little ability, knowledge and experience who somehow manage to blag themselves into a role way beyond their capabilities - when I was employed we used to call this, "being promoted to the level of your incompetence."

Do you really want to be like this though? Do you want your life to be a house of cards?

I don't. I'd be a nervous wreck.

Authentic self-belief is great to have but it's a bi-product of "know-how". If it's not then it's something else: it's a delusion. If you continually work at developing your skills, knowledge and abilities then the self-belief will take care of itself. You'll still need to take the time to recognise the valuable person you are developing into, but at least when you do look, you'll be hooking onto something solid, something real. Personal value naturally generates self-belief. And if you doubt yourself? Well, that might not necessarily be a bad thing. Perhaps it's telling you something.

In fact, sometimes a lack of self-belief can be a good thing, especially in the early stages of the goal achievement process. It's an indication that you need to step up; you need to push yourself into the unknown, get more experience and improve your skills and knowledge-base. It's there to keep you on your toes and can, in fact, be used as a powerful resource. I've met many successful people who are brilliant at what they do. They hold high, well-paid positions and are highly regarded yet doubt themselves every day. They use self-doubt to keep pushing themselves forward, as a reminder to keep learning and growing and not take liberties.

I'm not necessarily recommending this as a life strategy, but it does make you look at "self-doubt" in a different light. Maybe it doesn't have to be seen as a psychological disease that we have to eradicate. Perhaps it can be a powerful motivational force.

So when it comes to being successful, which quality do you think is more important?

Self-belief or know-how?

Or maybe that's entirely the wrong question? Perhaps it's more a case of relentlessly developing your know-how so that you become a person of high value that's almost impossible to not believe in.

CHAPTER 13

GETTING RESULTS EVEN WHEN YOU FEEL SHIT

"I didn't realise I had an anger problem until I took up golf!".

A couple of years ago I took up golf. It's a frustratingly beautiful game. You're only ever one shot away from disaster but, equally, you're only ever one shot away from thinking you're as good as Tiger Woods.

One of my friends - who is an exceptional golfer - used to regularly tell me that golf is the most psychological of all sports; if you play in a competition, you're out there on your own. You have to handle the pressure and, no matter what the game throws at you, somehow you have to take it on the chin and do your best to turn it into some kind of a positive. It can be brutally unforgiving if you allow it to be, but if your psychology is right, there's always the possibility to get something good out of a bad situation.

So, back to the opening line of this "thought":

"I didn't realise I had an anger problem until I took up golf".

It wasn't actually me who said that. It was a fellow golfer I was playing alongside recently in a competition. He said this right before he stormed off the course in a fit of rage because he'd messed up a single hole. My guess is, he's not going to become Scotland's equivalent of Tiger Woods. In fact, if he continues down this path, he's most likely not even going to have a consistently good amateur career, and there's a very obvious reason why: **he couldn't dig deep and find a way to get results when things were going shit.**

With any challenging activity we engage in, being able to handle adverse conditions is an essential skill. This is not just true with golf, it's true with most vocations. Perhaps it's an aspect of your career, business, or personal life. If you are required to perform regularly, there will inevitably be times where things don't quite go your way. And how you deal with these times is crucial to your consistency.

Do you manage to dig deep and pull out a result? Or do you have a meltdown like my golfing buddy?

There's a lot said in the world of self-help and personal development about creating a positive mindset; visualise precise success inside your mind; see a situation go exactly the way you would like it to go; do everything you can to make your inner visions a reality.

It's good practice to imagine success. It works well to have a positive focus and we do, in general, get more of what we place our attention on, in life. What often doesn't get much attention though, is the ability to imagine how we might react and respond when things **don't** go the way we envisage. And to then build in robustness to deliver results **even when** conditions aren't ideal. Irrespective of what we do, for a whole variety of potential reasons, spanners can get thrown in the works; perhaps we don't sleep well the night before a big presentation; or we eat something that doesn't agree with us; or we're struggling with a personal problem that keeps fighting for our attention. Does that mean we just give up because the conditions aren't ideal? I certainly hope not.

When you look at the lives of successful individuals you find that they regularly have to firefight. When Andy Murray won Wimbledon he was nursing all manner of niggling injuries. Personal development guru Tony Robbins has scarred his throat causing a significant voice problem but, on stage, he still somehow manages to convey the enthusiasm and intensity of a man possessed. The real skill of high achievers is often not their ability to consistently create the optimum environment to perform; their real skill is being able to find a way to produce great results **despite** the conditions being less than ideal.

Even if we have no wish to become an elite performer, we all still have to find a way to get results in less-than-desirable conditions. We need to cultivate a steeliness that makes it possible for us to dig out some kind of positive result, irrespective of the environment we find ourselves in. It's good to work at improving the environment, of course, but it's important we don't melt at the first sign of adversity. Our careers, our sanity, and our success depend on it.

I think this is an inevitable part of life and one that is often understated: the importance of being able to deliver **in spite** of how we feel. Or, to put in a more blunt way: **getting results even when things are shit**.

Some experiences, of course, can be so intensely negative that they knock us flat out and we'd be advised to take some time out, but the lesser negative experiences are ones we have to learn to deal with. That's why I'd like to recommend that you do a process called "devil's advocate testing". Whenever you set a goal for yourself, instead of just imagining it working out perfectly in your mind's eye, spend some time considering what might go wrong. I know this goes against the self-help rules of positive visualisation but it's a crucial part of the goal designing process. More importantly, though, it helps you appreciate the importance of pushing through adverse conditions: of getting results when things are shit.

When I'm playing golf, I know that there will be times where it seems like the golf-gods are conspiring against me. There are just too many variables to contend with. I do have influence over how I **respond** to these adverse situations though. So when I'm mentally preparing, I can run through these scenarios inside my mind, and creatively explore different ways to deal with them. Perhaps I'll imagine playing a bad shot and explore different ways to respond to it. Maybe I'll see myself just shrugging it off like a Zen Buddhist monk, or being excited by the prospect of exploring what I need to do differently. That way I'm factoring in the inevitable and teaching myself how to respond productively if, and when, the negative scenarios happen.

Imagining negative scenarios and exploring different ways to respond to them can be every bit as useful as envisioning your goals working out exactly the way you want them to. It creates flexibility but, above all, it helps build resilience to adversity - a steeliness that makes it possible for us to create sustainable results, irrespective of the negative situations we may encounter. It's a crucial life skill that often doesn't get the attention it deserves and one that's vital to creating consistency. It's important to take the bad with the good without melting: to dig deep and find a way to create something useful even when things are shit.

So what if, as well as dreaming about success, you also dreamt of failure? Not catastrophic failure, just some devil's advocate testing. Add in some challenges, some failures, and explore different ways to deal with them. By doing this, instead of teaching your mind that life is like a fairy tale, you'll be teaching it the importance of being robust. You'll also become someone who is flexible enough to change their approach when things aren't quite going the way you want them to.

A wonderful life is there to be created, that's for sure, but it also has to be managed.

CHAPTER 14

BE THE TORTOISE AND THE HARE

In practically every culture across the globe, there's the story of the fast and the slow. The classic version is the tale of the tortoise and the hare: The fictitious fable of a race between a boastful, arrogant hare and a quietly confident, plodding tortoise.

If you remember the story, you'll recall that the hare loved to self-advertise: to broadcast to all the other animals how unbelievably quick he was. Before the race, he stood confidently on top of a tree stump and boasted proudly that he had never been beaten; that he was, in fact, **un**beatable.

The tortoise, on the other hand, sat in the background, comfortable in the knowledge and appreciation of his own talents. He knew he had disadvantages over the hare but he also knew that, when it came to a longer race, he had a big advantage when it came to stamina. What he lacked in acceleration, pace and showmanship he more than made up for with dedication, longevity and persistence.

Both animals brought their respective attitudes and skills to the race. The hare shot off in a blaze of glory, dancing around like Mohammad Ali, as he put considerable distance between himself and the tortoise. He knew he was going to win. In fact, it was all a little bit insulting to his undoubted athletic dominance that the tortoise would even contemplate the possibility of victory.

The tortoise though wasn't overawed; he wasn't discouraged by the ever-increasing gap and the amateur dramatics displayed by the enigmatic hare. He just kept plodding along, doing the basics as well as he could. His focus was less on showing off to people how fantastic he was and more on demonstrating his talents through consistent and steady performance over a long period of time.

As I'm sure you recall from the story, the hare's arrogance and his overemphasis on showing off eventually becomes his undoing. While he's resting by a tree in the middle of the race, he becomes so relaxed and certain of his impending victory that he falls asleep. The tortoise - who has been quietly plodding away while the hare has been prancing around like a prize peacock - overtakes him and subsequently wins the race.

The hare wakes up, sees he has lost and is left scratching his head wondering what just happened. To the on-lookers though, it's obvious; he lost himself in his own arrogance and forgot the race was a marathon, not a sprint.

This tale is one that most parents tell their kids. The moral is simple and straight-forward: slow and steady wins the race. Success, in life, is a marathon, not a sprint. Embedded within the story is the idea that if you keep plodding along you'll reach your destination in the end and get your just rewards. Methodical consistency is more important than getting off to a dazzling fast start. Put simply: if you get the choice, be the **tortoise**, not the hare.

I find this an interesting idea to teach kids. It's solid advice. If you want to create anything worthwhile then it takes time, dedication and sustained hard work. But I'm also conflicted by it because it's starkly at odds with where the world is heading. Society at all levels is getting faster. The need for instant gratification and quick results is now firmly embedded in our consciousness.

We type in a question to Google and it'll supply us with thousands of answers in a fraction of a second. We obsess over the speed of our broadband and sometimes throw a fit when a website hangs up for more than 5 seconds. Netflix gives us a plethora of TV shows, on-demand. Amazon is considering hiring drones to deliver your parcels within a couple of hours because next day delivery isn't quite quick enough. Training courses are shorter than they used to be. Online learning is becoming more popular than ever because it allows us to learn "on-the-go".

Acquiring and achieving things quickly has made its way into the fabric of our being. We want things quickly and patience is rapidly becoming a lost virtue.

So while I think that the moral behind the fable of the tortoise and the hare is still important, it's perhaps not quite as all-encompassing as it once was. It's still as important as ever to be methodical, to think long-term and work towards developing sustainable skills and creating meaningful work. But we also need to live in the world that's presented to us. Consistency is crucial to success but so is making a quicker more dramatic impact. Life is still a marathon but, because of the way the world is, being able to show off our sprinting power is also something we have to become adept at doing.

That's why I think it's important that we tweak the story of the tortoise and the hare. It's not about choosing one or the other: it's important to be a bit of **both**.

We need to know how to methodically plod along at a constant, slow pace, but we also have to be able to ramp up the dazzle every now and again and show people how things can be done quickly. If not then they'll switch off.

You see an example of this in football (soccer) management. In days gone by coaches would get years to slowly build a team. Now they're lucky if they get a few months. So they're met with the challenge of having to create a sustainable level of results while at the same time dealing with the expectation of immediate success from the board and fans. They need to operate on both fronts. They have to get results quickly while at the same time build for the future.

If you run a business, it's important to have a long-term plan and methodically work your way towards it, but if you neglect the immediate cash flow you'll go under. As a business owner, you have to know how to get customers quickly, as well as building a solid, long-term infrastructure that will stand the test of time.

No matter what we do we have to be **both** the tortoise and the hare. We have to balance the quick and the slow.

So maybe we're telling the story the wrong way to our kids?

I'm not sure how the tortoise would get on in our fast-paced modern world. I think he'd most likely get mowed down by a motorbike-driving hare who's pre-occupied because he's too busy posting on Instagram while driving. We need to have an element of both the tortoise and the hare to be successful - make an impact while building for the future. It's the way of the world.

So how do you balance both?

What are you doing to create results now, and what are you doing to methodically build for the future?

How can you become a bit of both the tortoise and the hare?

Because your success depends on it.

SECTION 3

SELF-AWARENESS

CHAPTER 15

IF YOUR LIFE WERE A MOVIE, WHAT KIND OF MOVIE WOULD IT BE?

Last year I recommended a film to one of my friends – *Birdman*, starring Michael Keaton. He hated it so much he decided to send me an email. It was succinct and to the point, and simply said this:

"Your taste in films is shit. Birdman was crap…"

This hopefully tells you more about some of my friends than it does about my taste in films.

A couple of weeks later I bumped into him and we engaged in a healthy debate about movie preferences. Clearly, we had different tastes. It emerged that he liked faster-moving films, with powerful heroes and action-oriented plots, whereas I tended to go for more character-driven stories: ones with a slower pace that focused on developing the emotions and deeper intentions of the main characters. I did my best to convince him that he was missing out but it didn't work. Off he went to go watch the latest *Avengers* movie.

I'm not sure what Sigmund Freud would have said about the link between movie choice and a person's psychology but the discussion did get me thinking:

If your life were like a movie, what kind of move would it be? Would it be "plot" or "character" driven? Or something else?

Do you see it as an exciting, thrill-seeking, roller coaster of a ride like something starring Liam Neeson or Dwayne Johnson? Or is it one where the characters within it are more at the forefront? One that contains an array of interesting and deep personalities?

And do you find that your preference for films in any way reflects your personality and outlook on life?

For me, my choice of movies definitely resembles some of my life preferences and thinking styles. In general, I'm quite reflective, philosophical, and fascinated by human behaviour. I'm interested in the deeper motivations and mechanics of the human experience: why people do the things they do. It's perhaps no wonder that I like deeper, character-driven stories. I also like difference and uniqueness, and tend to get bored quickly when I see the same thing done over and over again in a similar, formulaic way - so you've probably guessed I'm not a big super-hero movie fan.

My aforementioned friend is starkly different. He prefers faster plots, all-out-action, and powerful heroes that have a drive for significance. If it's character-driven then it's too slow for him. He doesn't get it. If something hasn't been blown up within 5 minutes then he starts checking his phone.

Interestingly enough, he's not the most people-oriented person and seems to value "personal significance" quite highly. I'm not saying that there's a direct correlation but the similarities are quite interesting and potentially revealing.

Perhaps we could even expand this a little bit further and ask:

If your life was a style of movie, what style would that be?

A comedy? A rom-com? A thriller? A thoughtful drama? A work of fantasy?

I certainly hope it's not a disaster movie.

And what, if anything, might that say about the way you currently view life?

I'm not suggesting that this is some kind of pinpoint, accurate psychoanalysis that Freud would be envious of, but it is an interesting thing to reflect on, especially if an obvious pattern starts to emerge.

It might also be useful to look at it from a slightly different angle:

What would happen if you changed the types of movies that you watched?

What if you were to start watching films that were starkly different from those you currently watch?

Would that then have an effect on the way you experienced the world? Might it broaden your perspective?

Do you think it could open up areas of your experience that you weren't aware of before?

Personally, I think it would. If you ask any gifted storyteller or film director, they will tell you that a good film is not just meant to entertain, it's meant to expand the viewers' mind. Psychological enrichment is one of the often hidden, fundamental purposes of cinema.

So even if you don't quite buy into the idea that your movie choice reflects your personality, I'd like to suggest that you expand the choice of movies you see. Deliberately seek out different films that you wouldn't normally watch.

It's unconventional self-help advice I know, but I'm sure you'll find that it will make a big difference to how you view the world. You'll find that it subtly, and subconsciously, shapes and enriches your mind in a way that makes you a more well-rounded and resourceful person.

If you never watch films that are character driven, then commit to watching a few. If you never choose silly action moves and only watch serious, thoughtful dramas, then perhaps a nonsensical, shallow plot will do you some good? Who knows, perhaps my next movie will be *The Avengers*?

We learn by having different experiences so why shouldn't this also apply to films?

One of the most bizarre films I've ever seen is called *The Tribe*. It's a Ukrainian film set in a school for deaf children. The entire movie had no dialogue and all the characters used Ukrainian sign language to communicate - and there were no subtitles. It's not exactly the kind of film you'd expect to see at the top of the blockbuster list but it was absorbing. I was left feeling like my world had been expanded a little. Okay, maybe my taste in films is shit. Then again *The Tribe* wasn't my taste, but, after watching it, it is now. And that's the point.

So if your life were a movie, what kind of movie would it be?

And what would it be like if you expanded your choice and looked beyond?

You might just find that it makes a subtle, profound difference to your life.

CHAPTER 16

WHAT KIND OF INTERNAL SOUNDTRACK DO YOU HAVE?

Have you ever considered adding a soundtrack to your internal world?

Last year I went to see a silent movie in a theatre in Edinburgh. It was an old 1920s classic called, *The Cabinet of Dr Caligari*. Up until that point I hadn't been much of a fan of silent movies but this one made me change my mind. Technically, it wasn't completely silent. It had a soundtrack: A live pianist who had written a musical score specifically for the film.

I was blown away and sat mesmerised for the best part of 2 hours. The film itself stood up remarkably well - considering it was close to a hundred years old - but what elevated the experience was the musical score. There was something enchanting about it that had me hypnotised from the beginning to the end.

It made me think about how the soundtrack of a film

is often under-appreciated. Much of the emphasis goes on how it looks: the camera angles, lighting, facial expressions, and - especially with modern films - the special effects. When you tune in to the auditory elements though, you start to realise how important the musical score of a film is. It adds colour, shape and texture in a way that subtly, yet profoundly, affects both your emotional state and the meaning you attach to the scenes. The visuals may take the front seat, but the audio makes a powerful contribution from the background.

It's a bit like watching a sitcom that doesn't use canned laughter. Because you're not hearing other people laugh, it's harder to find the jokes funny. It's difficult to know if you should laugh or not.

This can also be true when it comes to our own inner subjective experience. If music - or lack of it - can make a profound difference to the level of engagement we experience in a film it can also make a difference to the level of engagement we experience in our inner world. By adding in our soundtrack of choice, we can create a more dynamic and interesting experience of life.

You might already do this; have you ever caught yourself humming out loud or playing a little tune inside your mind while doing the housework? Perhaps you even dance a little in time to the song, with your vacuum cleaner in hand? If you do, what effect does this have? I'm sure you'll find it almost always creates a subtle, yet definite, shift in your experience. It generally turns the mundane into something more interesting and enjoyable. Internal audio can be nearly as powerful in shaping how we feel and approach day-to-day life as external audio can in a movie.

So what - if any - internal soundtracks do you play?

What musical scores are part of your day-to-day inner world?

Perhaps you don't have any. Maybe the idea of imagining music playing inside your mind while you go about your day is something you've never considered before.

If this is a strange and alien concept to you then I recommend you try a few out. The fact that you don't currently do it most likely means that it will make a profound difference to your day-to-day experience of life. In the same way that a musical score makes a movie come alive, our own internal soundtracks can awaken a new type of experience inside of us. It can create a rhythm, a bit of drama, and generally makes the mundane more interesting - the "flat" and "dull" more vibrant and full of life.

Perhaps when you jump in the shower in the morning rather than looking in the mirror and moaning internally about how tired you are, you can hear the song *Eye of the Tiger* by Survivor instead.

Or maybe you'd like a dramatic cinematic moment: one that builds up to a crescendo - like Hans Zimmer's score in *Gladiator* - causing the hairs on the back of your neck to prickle with pride and inspiration?

Or perhaps you'd prefer something more serene: something minimalistic so that you can enjoy the silence between the thoughts? I often find that imagining something akin to classical music can work wonders for this. The baroque rhythms seem to inspire a calmness like no other sound can.

If you're looking for examples there are plenty out there. Just watch films, and pay attention to the music. When I was in my mid-thirties I used to regularly dance Cuban-style Salsa so I frequently had Latin music playing in my head. Just allowing a mix of different tracks to play inside my mind while I did the shopping, made the dinner, or did some housework transformed an uninspiring task into something much more engaging.

Nowadays - because of my aforementioned obsession with the era - I hear 80s music. Because I grew up in the 80s, it makes me feel young, fresh and energetic. There's so much choice. You're only limited by your imagination.

So, have a think: if you were to add in some profound soundtracks to your internal world which ones would you choose?

What would it be like if you made your internal world as engaging and inspiring as some of your favourite films?

Perhaps you could even hire your own imaginary pianist to create your very own unique musical score? The choice is yours.

CHAPTER 17

WHAT'S YOUR GLORIOUS OBSESSION?

In this thought, I'd like to talk about obsession. Not the perfume: the psychological mindset.

Obsession - or to be obsessed - is a curious one. It gets a lot of bad press, and often rightly so, but is it inherently bad? Can it also be a good thing?

We live in a world where everyone seems to have a certain amount of OCD (Obsessive Compulsive Disorder). Double-checking doors, looking at mobile phones for texts every two minutes, chronic worry, obsessing over finding the perfect partner, athletes with weird pre-performance rituals. There are examples everywhere you look. Obsession, while often being seen as an abnormality, actually seems to be quite, well, normal. Or at the very least common.

When people have an obsession that gets out of control they often go to their GP to seek help. If it's thought to be severe enough they then become "classified", labelled as someone who has a psychological disorder - as per the *DSM* (The Diagnostic Statistic Manual for mental illness).

Do they really have mental deficiency though? I'm not so sure.

There are clearly obsessive drives that get out of control and manifest themselves in highly destructive behaviours, and people who experience them do need help, but isn't the energy behind it all quite remarkable? Isn't it positive, natural and potentially useful if pointed in the right direction?

If you look at an entrepreneur who relentlessly pursues their goals, working 16-hour days for years on end; that's more than a little obsessive. If you watch a gourmet chef spend hours tinkering with the right way to present their food, moving a blade of lettuce a few millimetres to the right or left until satisfied, this fits most of the criteria for obsessive behaviour. So how are these examples different to someone who gets classified as an OCD sufferer because they feel compelled to clean for 12 hours a day?

The application and relationship to it is certainly different, but the energy behind the obsession is strikingly similar: we have something we desire and it's almost impossible to stop engaging with it.

As a business owner, I'm all too familiar with this. I have a consistent, compulsive need to want to continually develop and grow my business. I think about it all the time. I'm obsessed with it. But I enjoy it. I'm also obsessed with human psychology and have been for as long as I can remember. I'm constantly investigating human behaviour and I find that I have to stop myself talking about it in everyday conversations. I show all the signs of chronic mental deficiency. But I like it and wouldn't have it any other way.

There's a theory that obsession is, in fact, a natural human pattern. That if you look closely enough, everyone has the capacity to become obsessed about something. The potential for it is hard-wired in. If you look at professional athletes or those at the top of any profession, they are ludicrously obsessive. They can go to quite ridiculous lengths to control their body, training schedule and environment. They drill down to an obsessive level of detail in an attempt to etch out more of their potential.

Even in a non-professional setting, displaying obsessive behaviour is quite common. As someone who runs I've noticed that everyday, regular people can spend a fortune on getting the latest gear in an attempt to shave a few seconds off their personal best. Amateur golfers too; many of them obsess constantly over swing paths, choice of clubs and the latest technology.

So what's the difference between obsessions like these and ones that are debilitating problems requiring medication?

I'd like to suggest that the main difference lies not in the obsessive energy itself but in its application and the relationship people have with it. Is it a fundamental character flaw that requires psychiatric diagnosis? Perhaps. Or is it an energy that you can make friends with and re-direct to something positive? Personally, I choose the second.

Often the ferocious intensity behind obsession can be a little bit intimidating so some people "dissociate" from it and start treating it like they've been invaded by some kind of sinister alien force. They become disconnected from this powerful part of themselves, and an inner-struggle ensues. The internal battle then ups the stakes, increases the intensity of the obsession, and the relationship starts to deteriorate.

But when you appreciate that this drive is, in fact, a part of you, the intensity softens a little and you can start to aim it in a more useful direction. It becomes something that you can be friends with rather than a sinister nemesis attempting to wreak havoc on your well-being.

When you approach it in this way, this powerful drive can actually end up becoming something quite useful; something that leads to worthwhile, positive benefits.

For example, stop for a moment and imagine you were obsessed with being fit and healthy?

Or with learning?

Or reading?

Or becoming an excellent employee?

Or building a business?

Or becoming skilled in a crucial ability?

Or even being obsessed with living a meaningful life?

I'd say that these all have the potential to be positive, possibly glorious obsessions: ones that can make a positive and profound difference to our lives. Not ones that box us into a classification described in a manual for psychological disorders. It's still the same energy that exists behind the behaviour, but it's directed and managed in a much more ecological & healthy way.

So, to conclude the thought, I'd like to pose the question:

What could be your glorious obsession?

What, in your life, would you like to relentlessly pursue that would make you happier, healthier and more enriched?

If we all have the potential to be obsessed why not make use of it? There's great power there and, when we make friends with it, we can point it in the direction of making our lives immeasurably better.

So which parts of your life would you like to make obsessively better?

CHAPTER 18

THE OVER-CORRECTION

I'm addicted to the TV series *How I Met Your Mother*. While watching an episode recently, I found that it revealed a rather profound insight into human behaviour. The episode was entitled, "the over-correction" and was based on the idea that, as human beings, we have a tendency to swing from one extreme to the other; especially when emotional intensity is involved. If an important area of our life doesn't quite work out the way we'd like it to then we run the risk of taking huge action and over-correcting.

In the episode in question, they focused on dating. For example, say you dated someone who is a bit of a bad-boy, or bad-girl, and it ends badly, there will be a natural urge to want to minimise risk in your next relationship: to over-correct by going to the other extreme. Perhaps you'll date someone who's "just a bit too safe", in an attempt to fulfil the elements that the previous relationship lacked.

I found the episode fascinating because I think it's a

strategy that many people adopt. When we're disappointed with the results we get, within an important area of our life, it's hard to resist the urge to demonise the current approach and opt for something wildly different: to be bipolar in our decision making and swing dramatically from one extreme to the other. And this is almost **never** a good idea. Every approach will come with positives and negatives so by over-correcting we lose out, almost entirely, on the benefits that one side has to offer.

Perhaps you hate your job because you get little time off so you quit and get a part-time one – or retire – so you have plenty of time to do your own thing. Then after 6 months, you realise that you're bored out of your mind.

Or the opposite: your job contains little in the way of stimulation so you take a promotion, load yourself up with more responsibility than you can handle, only to realise that you actually quite like having time and space every now and again.

Or maybe you were super skinny as a teenager so you decide to beast yourself every day in the gym to build muscles and end up struggling to fit through a standard sized door.

Or perhaps you were overweight as a teenager and now

you're unhealthily obsessed with food, your weight and your looks, counting every calorie as if your life depends on it.

These are all examples of over-corrections: where we swing from one extreme to another because of an intense negative experience.

It's not just our behaviour this affects either. Over-corrections work from an emotional perspective too. In therapy, people who have experienced trauma can make the decision to go completely numb emotionally, to protect themselves from future pain. In relationships, some people can be hurt so badly by the betrayal of a partner that they decide to "never love again". In the workplace, some employees can become apathetic and uncaring because they've experienced prolonged stress.

Reactions like these are completely understandable but it's important to realise that, while they do provide a certain sense of short-term security, the long-term negative consequences are enormous. To "not feel", "not love", or "not care" are big prices to pay. Over a longer period of time, it's we who end up losing out on a richer experience of life.

I'm not saying that it's easy to overcome emotional events like these, because it's not. I'd just like to encourage people to be more aware of the over-corrections they are choosing to do. To over-correct is a natural urge, and with some situations it's necessary, especially in the short-term. When we play the long-game though, it's not the best strategy for healthy living. It ultimately ends up **restricting** choice rather than **expanding** it, and it can often create a destructive "yo-yo" effect.

I have a friend who regularly swings from one dramatic extreme to the other: He is either a borderline alcoholic who eats McDonalds and takeaways several times a week while doing no exercise, or he's a teetotal, salad eating, exercise maniac. He's become better with age but he's been running this pattern of swinging from one extreme to the other for close to 10 years now, and it's certainly not helped him with sustained weight loss or become healthier.

Sometimes having a dramatic swing in our life is **absolutely** required but most of the time we can end up just creating a different kind of problem when we hit the other end of the spectrum. Usually, the "sweet-spot" of human experience is somewhere between the two extremes, incorporating elements of each side. You might end up closer to one side than the other, and in a much different place than you started, but rarely does it involve the complete exclusion of the opposite.

So have a think:

Where do you over-correct? Or where have you over-corrected in the past?

It's not necessarily a bad thing. Like I say, sometimes in life we do have to make a dramatic swing and do something starkly different to what we currently do. But if we do this regularly it can end up just creating another layer of problems when we hit the other end of the spectrum. Life is rarely black-and-white but rather a continuum of infinite variations, so it's often a poor choice to treat it in such a bi-polar way. Instead, look for a way to incorporate a bit of both sides of the coin. Create more balance.

How can you have an exciting relationship that also has an element of safety?

How can you eat healthily while at the same time occasionally enjoying a few vices?

How can you exercise in a way that also allows your body time to repair?

How can you embrace strength and vulnerability at the same time?

Start to see life more as a sliding scale, with a wide variety of different choices, rather than a straight decision between one extreme or the other. See if you can find your own sweet-spots.

So what's it like when you widen your inner picture frame to include elements of both sides?

What's it like when you "correct" your over-correction?

CHAPTER 19

THE POWER OF "EXPECTATION"

Have you ever considered the power that "expectation" can have in shaping your outlook on life? How it can affect your mood, motivation, and sense of fulfilment?

Expectation is an interesting concept. It's where we have a strong belief about what will happen to us, or how a situation will play out. We don't often realise it - because they frequently work at a subconscious level - but our expectations play a crucial part in shaping our experience.

I'm a big football fan - or soccer if you're in the USA or Australia. I'm also Scottish so I do my patriotic bit by feverishly supporting the national team when they play. At the time of writing, the Scottish team had just played a key match against Israel in the Nations League. A lot was at stake since winning would mean promotion to a higher division and a play-off place for the European championships.

My expectations when watching Scotland tend to be

exceptionally low. Years of painfully watching them choke spectacularly when the pressure is on has caused me to be extremely cautious with my optimism. As a football team, we seem to be experts at grabbing defeat from the jaws of victory, continually finding new ways to torture expectant fans. It's truly a talent. So I was pleasantly surprised when they won and got through to the next round of a group competition for the first time in Scottish footballing history. What followed for me, in the 30 minutes after the game, can only be described as a feeling of euphoria; pure bliss and elation.

I'm aware that this possibly makes me sound a little primitive and tribal but, honestly, try supporting a team that consistently, over decades, gives you continual glimmers of hope only to whip them away at the last minute, leaving you crushingly disappointed. You tend to celebrate the important victories on the rare occasions they happen.

The most important thing I found about this experience though, is the role that my own expectations had on producing such a dramatic reaction: I expected very little but got a lot more.

There are a number of things that generally have to come together to produce a feeling of euphoria but one of the factors is often to do with the "expectation" we set beforehand. When something considerably exceeds our expectations we get a jolt of pleasure. When it's also something meaningful to us this jolt can often tip into ecstasy. Bliss. Elation. Euphoria.

It can also work the other way round: disappointment does require **adequate planning**. To be disappointed, we have to create an expectation of what we'd like to happen beforehand and then fall short. The feeling doesn't just magically occur, there's a build-up.

Expectations can also be profoundly motivating. Have you ever been in a situation where somebody important expects you to deliver? Like your boss, a close friend or family member? I'm sure you felt a mildly uncomfortable desire to take action. In situations like these, we often go above and beyond the call of duty to deliver; someone we respect expects a certain standard so we go the extra mile.

As a coach myself, I appreciate that this is one of the fundamental principles that all successful one-to-one coaching is based upon. A skilled coach should be ambitious for their clients and this ambition is often actualised by continually ramping up the level of expectation. Expectation creates accountability, and that accountability leads to action. It gets people to move.

Then there's the less well-known relationship we have with expectation: the trick of "released expectation". We often forget that we don't necessarily have to have any expectation at all. We can choose to let go and release our expectations to the extent where we are simply open to explore and see what happens. In fact, from working with a few top performers this is often the last step they do to flip themselves into peak performance - especially in sports or the performing arts. They place colossal expectations on themselves to prepare methodically for an event, but when the event arrives they let go and release all expectations so that they can relax and slip fully into the moment.

It sounds counter-intuitive but it makes sense when you think about it. To perform at a high level you have to put pressure on yourself to prepare extensively, which is done through raising your level of expectation. But when it comes to delivering on the day, you need to relax and focus fully on the present. By releasing all your expecta-tions your attention is taken away from your future goals causing you to focus on the here-and-now.

It's like the quote I once heard on the TV from

world-famous sprinter Michael Johnson. He said, "If you're about to try to win the school county championships then you don't want to be thinking about winning the Olympics. Focus on the job at hand." Releasing expectations allows us to do that.

Expectations can come in many shapes and forms, and getting to grips with them can be a profoundly useful skill to develop. They're not some mysterious force that just happens: we create them.

So what about you? How do you currently manage your own expectations? Or perhaps it's something you've never thought about.

If it's not then I'd recommend doing so now. There are lots of options available; you can lower or raise the stakes depending on what you want to experience.

Do you want to feel wonderfully surprised and elated? Then lower your expectations.

Do you want to achieve more? Then increase your expectations. Expect more from yourself and hold yourself accountable. Or better still get a coach. If they're good they'll be ambitious for you. This will increase the demands that you place on yourself but you'll also get more back from life.

Or perhaps you'd like to try letting go of expectations completely for a portion of time? Releasing the need to achieve a certain result and simply explore. This can be wonderfully zen-like and therapeutic, and can also help you be more present and in the moment.

Personally, I like to have three modes: when I need to work and prepare I place high expectations on myself; when I need to perform I let go of these expectations so I can be in the moment; and when I'm enjoying downtime and recreation I lower my expectations. How you do it though, is up to you.

So I'd suggest that in the coming week you turn your attention to the level of expectation that you place on yourself, and how it fluctuates depending on the situation. And from there you can experiment, playing about with different modes. Find what works for you.

It takes practice of course, but I **expect** that it will be all worth the effort.

CHAPTER 20

THE EFFORT SWEET SPOT:
PSYCHOLOGICAL CLUTCH CONTROL

One of the world leaders in personal development is American self-help guru Tony Robbins. If you've never heard of him do a Google search. The first thing that will strike you will be the size of his teeth. The second thing will be the amount of energy he puts out during his seminars and talks. It's close to super-human.

Tony has a simple philosophy that's central to all of his work: he calls it "playing all-out". It's based on the belief that the secret to success, achievement, peak performance, and ultimately life-fulfilment, is to throw everything at it. Take every bit of energy, effort and vitality you have and fire it like the world's most intense laser beam everywhere you go. Learn to "play all out" in every aspect of your life. Leave nothing off the pitch.

This idea is not just isolated to Tony's work. It seems to be intrinsically linked with success, achievement and fulfilment in most areas of life: that to be a high achiever you have to continually access unfathomable amounts of adrenalin, effort and intensity. The more the better. You have to push, strive, and be driven. Become an unstoppable force and create your compelling future through sheer-force-of-will.

I think this is good advice: if you want to kill yourself.

It is true up to a point, of course. Succeeding at anything does require hard work continually applied over a long period of time. It does require that we put in a significant amount of effort. We do, in general, get out of life what we put in.

There comes a point though, where this philosophy flips on its head and – counter-intuitively - starts to work against us. As we continually up our efforts - doubling, tripling or quadrupling our intensity - in an attempt to make our dreams a reality, we eventually reach a threshold: an upper limit where, beyond it, the world starts to push back. Instead of getting more back for our input we get less. The extra effort is not only wasted, but it also begins to work against us. In other words, we end up just trying too damn hard!

One of the most obvious places to see this in action is on the dating scene. If you've ever been single for longer than you would like to be, I know you will have had an experience like this. Nothing seems to flip you over the effort threshold quicker than feeling like you'll be "left on the shelf". Suddenly, your opportunities seem limited so you up your efforts, try that bit harder, only to find that your actions seem to be **repelling** people rather than attracting them. You feel like you're working so damn hard but getting little back in return.

Or perhaps you meet someone who fits most of your relationship criteria and you start acting like a total weirdo. Through a combination of nerves and fear of missing out you start trying to push things too hard and too quick, forcing the conversation when you first meet them rather than allowing it to naturally flow. Maybe you also start projecting far off into the future, to the point when you're married, have two kids named Gerald and Siobhan, and a lovely suburban lifestyle: all of course, before you've even been on the second date.

Even if you haven't done this yourself, I know that you'll have heard of someone who has. The problem isn't caused by a lack of effort: it's caused by too much.

This is not solely exclusive to dating either. It's a natural phenomenon that affects us in practically every walk of life:

invest more energy and effort than is naturally required and friction is created, one that decreases performance, causes the world to push back, and ultimately makes our goals much more difficult to achieve than what they need to be.

So what, then, is the solution? If putting in too much effort can create a problem, then what should we do instead? Nothing? Should we just sit back, visualise success and then wait for the universe to deliver?

Of course not.

The solution lies somewhere in between. Rather than trying to always max out your efforts relying solely on intensity, the key is to find your effort sweet spot - the place where you're investing **just the right amount** of effort and energy to move forward without much in the way of wastage. Not too much, not too little. Rather than throwing yourself about with the intensity of an amphetamine addict, find that place where you slip into the natural ebb-and-flow of your world. Where life becomes a dance rather than something you're attempting to dominate through sheer force of will.

We need to invest effort into our goals and dreams - with some goals requiring more than others - but we also need to know when to let go. Taking the foot **off** the gas can be just as important as putting the foot on it. By learning to skillfully balance both effort and letting go, we can hit our own sweet spots that make it possible for life to flow.

I think, for me, one of the most visually obvious examples I've witnessed of people hitting this sweet spot, was when I went to see the Edinburgh Marathon as a teenager. Generally, you don't see much: just swarms of people hurtling past you, some faster than others, with many wearing all kinds of weird and wonderful costumes.

What caught my attention though, were the leaders: the way they moved. It was like watching a herd of beautiful gazelles glide past at frightening speed. They were jogging faster than I could sprint yet it all looked so effortless. They were, of course, putting plenty of effort in, but their body dynamics and mental state were coordinated in such a way that it seemed like they had locked into some kind of smooth, mesmeric, effortless rhythm.

You couldn't take your eyes off them. They had found a way of using their body and mind to get the optimum level of performance from the minimum amount of effort; to slot into the natural rhythm of their world rather than trying to force and dominate it. Whatever it was they were doing, they had clearly found their own physical and psychological sweet spot.

Another example of this kind of **effort efficiency** is the tennis player Roger Federer. While he was enjoying almost utter dominance in the sport, he frequently dispatched his opponents with ease, hardly looking like he had moved out of second gear. At the end of his matches, it looked like he'd barely broken a sweat. He had just run around a court for the best part of 3 hours but, in his after-match press conference, it was as if he'd just nipped out for a Sunday morning paper. His colossal success was never down to putting in maximum effort all the time; he had mastered the ability of using his energy efficiently. He was operating from his effort sweet spot.

I don't think this phenomenon is something that restricts itself to elite sport either, it's something that comes into play in practically every aspect of our life. No matter what we do, whether it be through our external behaviours or our psychological thinking, there will always be a sweet spot with regards to the amount of effort and energy we invest. Get close to it and it can feel like we are floating through life, creating exquisite results from a place of flow. Go significantly above it though, and it starts to feel like one big slog and our results are diminished.

Think about it: if you were to recall a time when everything just flowed, did it feel like you were working hard? Or did it feel like you were investing just the right amount of energy to fit the needs of the situation? I find it's almost always the latter.

The effort threshold can be seen in many different areas of life. Here are a few everyday examples that hopefully you can relate to:

- **Exercise**: When we go to the gym to get fitter and stronger, the improvement doesn't happen when we work out. We become fitter and stronger when we rest. Put too much effort in by overtraining and we'll eventually break down. With exercise, rest days are just as important as training days.

- **Sustainable success**: If we're working on a long-term project it's important to pace ourselves. Some people - especially if the project is important - will try to work 14 hours a day, 6 days a week only to collapse and get ill halfway through. The excessive schedule becomes counter-productive because it impairs their cognitive sharpness and prevents them from performing at a high level. To improve long-term performance they need to reduce the effort they're putting in.

- **Psychological**: Sometimes, if we are experiencing a problem, we can think too hard about the solution. The harder we try to figure it out the less sense it seems to make and everything starts to fizzle out. When we take the foot off the gas though, and allow things to settle, we can often get insights into the situation - how many times have you had an "Aha!" moment in the bath?

- **Social**: Sometimes if we want to make a good impression, it can be easy to force ourselves into conversations, perhaps in an attempt to get people to like us. The conversation can then become forced and unnatural. Good social interaction has a rhythm to it; an ebb and flow.

- **Leadership**: Sometimes leaders can push their team too far, neglecting their needs, energy levels and capabilities. This can cause pushback, de-motivation, or worse: a revolt!

Whether or not these examples fit with you, I'm sure you get the idea: we need to invest effort to get something moving but too much can work against us. "Playing all out" in every aspect of your life is not good advice. And you don't always get out what you put in.

It's vastly more important to find your **effort sweet spot**. That magical place where life becomes a dance, and you find the balance between going for it and allowing things to naturally develop. It's in this place that you can make the most of what you do while at the same time minimising pushback. It's where life begins to naturally flow.

So, what's your effort sweet spot? Where is that place for you when you're applying just enough force that causes you to slip into the natural ebb-and-flow of experience?

It can change from situation to situation of course, but in general, what works for you? Do you have a tendency to put too much effort in? Or too little? What adjustments could you make to get close to your sweet spot?

Finding your balance can often be like doing clutch control in a car on a hill. Effective clutch control is about developing a sense as to the amount of pressure that's required to be applied to both the clutch pedal and the accelerator, at the same time, in order to balance and control the car. Too much or too little either way then the sweet spot is lost, and the car either stalls or starts to act like a bucking bronco at a rodeo show.

It can often be a similar experience when it comes to finding the effort sweet spots in our life. It's not about pushing hard all the time - or not pushing at all - it's about finding just the **right** amount of pressure, the right balance between pushing and letting go. Just enough to bring out the best in you, and those you interact with, but not so much that you, or they, become overwhelmed, running the risk of physical, psychological or social breakdown.

Some situations will clearly require a high amount of pressure and exertion, while others will require less. The key thing is to be aware and remain flexible: to test, gauge and adjust. Find that spot where conscious effort and personal intention are in balance with the natural rhythm of the social and environmental world.

Finding our own effort sweet spots can be one of the most rewarding things we can do, for our performance, success, sense of fulfilment, and our physical and psychological health.

What would it be like if you found your sweet spots more often?

Perhaps it would make life sweeter than you can possibly imagine.

CHAPTER 21

DON'T BECOME A TESTOSTERONE-FUELLED MALE BEING WHIPPED IN A BAR

"You don't want to be a blind-drunk, testosterone-fuelled male being whipped in a bar."

I said this line to a friend of mine recently when we were discussing the power of the mind. We were talking about "mind-over-matter": the ability to use your mind to override physical symptoms such as pain, discomfort or even unwanted emotional sensations. He is a cyclist and regularly waxes-lyrical about the incredible feats that elite cyclists overcome in events such as the Tour de France. Even as part of their training they practically destroy their bodies to force it into quite inhumane levels of fitness.

He was remarking about how important it is in life to fight through the pain barrier: to push yourself beyond the limits of your body's endurance. You only get out what you put in so every day you should play life at 120%.

As we chatted, - as well as internally chastising him for being ignorant at maths - I was mentally transported back to my early 20s to a time when I was on a holiday in Majorca with my friends. As a Scot, it appears to be a rite of passage to go off to a Brit-infested holiday resort once a year and get miraculously drunk for a week, so this particular memory was, unsurprisingly, situated in a bar.

All of sudden the music stopped and the DJ announced that he was looking for two men and women to take part in a bar competition with the prize being a free nights alcohol.

The game was simple but brutal: the women were given a wide variety of instruments such as whips, belts and large boxing gloves and they were to take turns inflicting mild to moderate pain on the men. The man who managed to last the longest number of rounds won the prize. It's difficult to accept that someone would be foolish enough to volunteer for something like this but they were inundated with offers. It just goes to show what some drunk, testosterone-fuelled males will do when in front of an audience.

A gruesome hour later, one of the men - apparently he was a kickboxer - stood victorious, with his chest and stomach covered in bruises, and what looked like a seriously damaged collar bone in urgent need of medical attention. A man next to me turned around with a rather crazed and excited look on his face and said, "That was incredible! Isn't it wonderful what 'mind-over-matter' can achieve?"

Yes…isn't it just.

Or, is it really?

So it was the reminiscing of this past event that caused me to utter the aforementioned line to my friend, as a word of warning. Hopefully, he got my intended message. Mind-over-matter: it's not all it's cracked up to be.

Now don't get me wrong, sometimes we need to push beyond our limits; sometimes we need to dig deep and struggle on, irrespective of pain and suffering. Overcoming adversity - both physical and psychological - is a vital skill in life. It's how we create consistency. But if we play "all-out" every day of life we'll become a spent force pretty soon. And if you play life at 120%? Well, you should book yourself in for some maths tuition but that's a different point. In special circumstances, we **do** have to override our natural defences, but for the most part, the opposite approach is a lot more important: the ability to **listen** to our body and work **with** it.

If we push too hard, for too long, eventually our body

will respond. It **will** escalate things to a higher level and who knows what that might be. Listening to our body, and the signals it provides, is one of the most important things we can do when it comes to creating more inner and outer harmony. Sometimes those signals can be loud and clear whereas other times they can be more subtle. But they can be felt and heard if we practice turning our attention to them.

Our body and mind are one unit, working intricately together, yet we so often treat them as separate entities. In fact, even the idea of mind-over-matter contains the implication that the two are competing with each other for dominance. It's a horrible frame to put around it and just creates unnecessary conflict.

So instead of trying to use your mind to dominate your body, I'd like to encourage you to develop the opposite: to work with your body and improve the relationship you have with it: to listen, to feel, to acknowledge, to take into consideration and to understand. It's important to bridge the gap between cognition and physicality in order to create a more harmonious relationship.

I'd also extend this to emotions. Emotions are, after all, merely interpretations of what we feel; it's where we mix cognition with physical sensation. Almost always, a significant part of any psychological problem we experience is the damaged relationship we create with our emotional being. It's often our reaction to the horrible feeling rather than the feeling itself that's the biggest issue. The feeling itself is a message from within; it's highlighting what we are responding to. It's only when we acknowledge this and start to explore with curiosity that we can work with it; we can accept, negotiate or even re-direct the energy.

So instead of attempting to dominate your physical and emotional experience through mental processes, try doing the opposite: work at improving the connection you have with yourself. Feel more. Listen more. Acknowledge. Work with. Re-direct. You might still decide to go and do something that conflicts with its wishes anyway, but at least you're paying attention. At least you're working from the premise that the Mind-Body - or Body-Mind - is one combined entity.

Your body will understand, up to a point, providing it knows you're listening. Providing it's been welcomed to the party. Just don't ignore it. Because trust me on this: the last thing you want, is to be a blind-drunk, testosterone-fuelled male being whipped in a bar.

CLOSING WORDS

From tortoises and hares and *Back to the Future*, to character-driven films and testosterone-fuelled males being whipped in bars, we've been on a journey together. And isn't that what life is like: a journey? One that can be as random and unpredictable as it is structured and organised.

I certainly hope you've enjoyed our journey, and that you've experienced some interesting insights and shifts in perspective along the way. If not, then maybe there are revelations that are yet to bubble up from beneath and arrive at a level that's conscious to you. Sometimes insight can be like this.

If you found some of the thoughts a little bit "jarring" then I'd suggest that that's a good thing. Often when we are encouraged to think about something from a different perspective our beliefs are challenged, and it can feel a little bit disorientating. That's perfectly normal so just go with it. Personally, I love this because I know that it means that my mind is being expanded, but I know, for some, it can be a little bit unsettling. If that's the case for you, then just give it time to settle and see where it goes. It's a good indication that the process of re-evaluation has been set in motion. You are also, of course, fully entitled to disagree with my opinions. I won't take it personally.

Ultimately though, it's my wish that this book has helped you think differently about life. As the old self-help adage goes, "If we always do what we've always done, then we'll always get what we've always got." We need to continually evolve and change with the world, and the way to do this is by exploring "difference". Different behaviours. Different activities. Different ways of thinking. And this all starts when we step into a new and different perspective.

Hopefully, you have also coped with - and enjoyed - the slightly random nature of the book. It's good to have a self-help system that leads you from step 1 to step 10 in a nice orderly fashion, but it's also important to appreciate that much of the way we live and think is mildly chaotic and random: organic and unpredictable. And often it's this unpredictable nature that can make life so surprisingly beautiful and fulfilling.

I remember an example of this that stuck with me from a few years ago. It was during a time where we were having a dreadful winter with excessive snow falls. All across Scotland, households had several feet of snow lying in their gardens and streets, and it was causing complete and utter chaos.

I remember my street being particularly bad, to the extent where we were getting frequent power failures. During one long power cut, I started to get frustrated from not being able to find any matches to light my candles, so I decided to take a trip down to my local supermarket. One thing I've found that you can always rely on, most likely even during a Zombie apocalypse, is that a large supermarket chain will somehow manage to find a way to stay open.

I put on my heavy-duty winter gear and started the hike in the snow. Half an hour later I arrived and they hadn't disappointed. Lit up like a Christmas tree, most likely with some kind of post-apocalyptic emergency back-up power generator, was the 24-hour store that would simply not be beaten by a few million flakes of snow and a national grid power-cut.

I entered and headed over to the cigarette counter to

buy some matches. I'm not exactly sure what happened next but, after about 15 minutes, I found myself wandering around the clothing section eying up a rather fetching leather jacket. It was like I had been hypnotised. In reality, though, I'd just wandered off my pre-determined route and started to do a bit of meandering. I took off my winter coat and tried the jacket on. It looked great. It was super cool and fitted me perfectly.

I wandered out, ecstatically happy, with my unexpected purchase and started my journey back home. It wasn't until I got about a hundred paces from the store that I realised what I had done: I'd become so engrossed in the jacket that I'd completely forgotten to buy the boxes of matches. Cursing my forgetfulness I hauled myself back in, quickly bought them, then returned back to my journey home in the snow.

As I strolled back through the blizzard it occurred to me how insignificant the matches now seemed to be; I was too busy enjoying the happiness of my new cool jacket to care. My initial reason for heading out into the wild winter was now a distant thought, replaced instead with something that ultimately turned out to be far more enjoyable and worthwhile.

It's interesting how that can happen sometimes. We go for one thing in life and end up getting something unexpected that's even more fulfilling. I think that's what can happen when we randomise our life a little. When we briefly step away from systems and procedures and just explore.

I'm not suggesting that all of life is like buying a cool leather jacket while you're trying to purchase matches, but some of it is. Random, unexpected journeys can produce some beautiful moments.

So I do hope that your journey into the random scribbles of my mind have produced some unexpected, yet enriching moments for you. I wish you all the best for the future and hope that you have many more transformational, therapeutic thoughts.

ABOUT THE AUTHOR

Steven Burns is a therapist, coach, trainer and writer. He is the creator of *Solutions in Mind*, a personal development organisation that offers psychological solutions to everyday problems. He has created multiple online learning programmes to help people make tangible, concrete transformations in their life. More than 35, 000 students have enrolled in his courses, spanning over 164 countries. He regularly gives talks and seminars and delivers several different live accreditation programmes throughout the year.

To get in touch with Steven,
email him at: **info@solutionsinmind.net**.

Printed in Great Britain
by Amazon